SURREY
TALES OF MYSTERY
AND MURDER

SURREY
TALES OF MYSTERY
AND MURDER

W. H. Johnson

COUNTRYSIDE BOOKS
Newbury, Berkshire

First published 2002
© W. H. Johnson 2002

COUNTRYSIDE BOOKS
3 Catherine Road
Newbury, Berkshire

To view our complete range of books,
please visit us at
www.countrysidebooks.co.uk

ISBN 1 85306 743 1

Designed by Mon Mohan

Produced through MRM Associates Ltd., Reading
Printed by J. W. Arrowsmith Ltd., Bristol

Contents

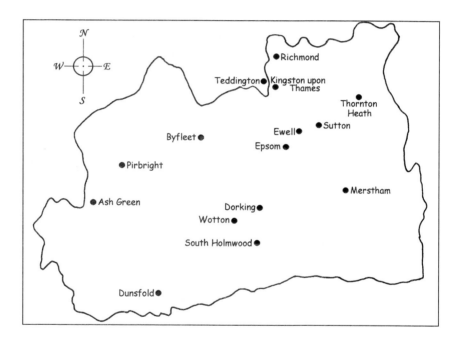

Introduction

In this selection of murders and mysteries I have striven to assemble as wide a variety of material as possible.

Three of the murders may be described as classics of their kind. Vaquier, the vain little Frenchman who poisoned a man who thought him a friend, will for many more years continue to be recalled for the cold-blooded dreadfulness of his offence as will Whiteway, the towpath killer, and the despicable bank robber, Michael Hart.

Several of the murders are themselves quite powerfully mysterious, still carrying with them their unanswered questions. For instance, why was a perfectly ordinary newsagent with no apparent enemies shot to death in his shop one early morning? And why did two brothers from a wealthy home pick up an unsuspecting water board official, take him to a wood and murder him? Even though the men were apprehended their motive is still not known. Then there is the classic mystery of Sophia Money, flung to her death off a train. But why and by whom?

I have included the astonishing account of the poltergeist at Thornton Heath. What a mystery that is and yet the careful records made by professional researchers leave no doubt about the genuineness of this remarkable affair. And how are we to account for the experience of a man and his wife who went on a Sunday trip to the country? Did they really step into another time and another place? And can a ghost really be conjured up and thrive on the animosities of a man and his wife?

But I am not going to lay a complete trail of questions to entice you to read the following pages. Let me just say that I hope that you will read them and that you will find them intriguing.

Johnnie Johnson

Acknowledgements

In researching this book I have had to rely very much, as always, on the helpfulness of others. I am particularly grateful to the staffs of Surrey History Centre, Sutton Library, Epsom Library, Ewell Library and Croydon Local Studies Library.

I should also like to offer my warmest thanks to Edward Shortland whose original research into the 1919 riot at Epsom was exceptionally helpful; to Paul Williams whose newspaper cuttings service, Murder Files, has as usual saved me much footslogging; to Ken Money for his observations on the draft of the Merstham Tunnel Murder chapter; to Muriel O'Grady of Ash for her contribution to the Ash Manor story and to Sally Jenkinson for kindly permitting me to use the photograph of Ash Manor; and to my old friends Brian and Jenny Richards whose chase after wild geese was very much appreciated.

Finally I should like to acknowledge the help I have received from my wife, Anne. As ever with my books, she has cast a critical eye over the drafts and has made not only valuable but vital criticisms about both style and content. I am more grateful to her than I may sometimes appear.

THE THORNTON HEATH
POLTERGEIST

You'd think that poltergeists would be more considerate, wouldn't you? You'd think at least that they might observe normal hours especially when people are ill. But when a poltergeist disturbance started up in Thornton Heath, convenience counted for nothing. The fact that it was nearly midnight and that Leslie and Alma Fielding had been confined to bed for the last three days, he having had all his teeth out earlier in the week – they did that sort of thing in 1938 – and she with her usual serious kidney trouble, was ignored. There in the dark, over in the corner of the bedroom, was what sounded like glass smashing and when Alma switched on the light there before their eyes a tumbler flew across the room and shattered against the wall.

The noise from the bedroom roused the lodger, George Saunders, and 16 year old Donald Fielding. They both dashed into the bedroom only to see the eiderdown lift off the bed and swathe itself over the heads of Leslie and Alma. Before anyone had recovered from that surprise the bedroom light went out and try as they might they were unable to switch it on. Finally, by the light of a torch, they saw that the bulb had been removed from its socket and placed on a chair. The bulb was still too hot to handle.

And so, on 18th February 1938, began the classic poltergeist haunting of a most respectable house in Beverstone Road in Thornton Heath. For the next two or three weeks there was what might be described as a poltergeist spectacular at the Fieldings' end of terrace house, which attracted the attention of the local and national press – there were even several foreign journalists who presented themselves at the house – and daily the crowds outside pressed themselves forward in the hope of glimpsing just one of the occupants and had to be held in check by the police. It was so important a story that the *Croydon Advertiser* permitted one of its reporters – unfortunately unnamed – to accept the Fieldings' invitation to spend several days in the house. For the first few days mediums from throughout the district came to proffer solutions, while officers of the International Institute for Psychical Research not only visited Beverstone Road but then conducted a serious four-month study of the events. The IIPR reports are contained in two bulky files, now lodged at the library of the University of Cambridge. As poltergeist disturbances go, those at Thornton Heath were of profound interest.

The disturbance which had begun late at night in the Fieldings' bedroom seemed to peter out quite quickly. Later next day, however, there were further irrationalities. Against all the laws of natural science, an egg launched itself through the air and broke on the sideboard; then it was the turn of ornaments, cups, saucers and yet more glasses to waltz round the room before breaking against the walls and floors of bedrooms, kitchen and dining room. A glass, one of a set locked up in the sideboard, smashed itself against the fender – yet the sideboard doors remained locked. A cup and saucer in Alma Fielding's hand crumbled into thousands of pieces.

And the cause? Perhaps it was Donald. Young people were often the focus of poltergeist eruptions. Mediums who had been holding a seance in the house suggested that he was in peril and that he ought to leave the house and stay in some less dangerous place. Yet for some days Donald remained where he was. Perhaps that was because, in spite of everything that he had seen in the last twenty-four hours, his father Leslie was unable to take the matter seriously. Sceptical about such matters, he was convinced that there must be a rational explanation. Plain, matter of fact people like Leslie Fielding do sometimes take some convincing. On the other hand, the attractive 35 year old Alma was curious about what was happening, fascinated by it all, and in the succeeding weeks even her health and appearance improved as the affair became increasingly interesting to her.

On the Sunday there were further inexplicable occurrences and by the Monday the family were obliged to summon police protection because so great was the publicity that the crowds were trying to force their way into the house. But the Fieldings were pleased to invite the *Advertiser* man to be their guest. How fortunate he felt himself to be there. What a story this was. An egg cup seemingly out of nowhere broke into fragments at his feet. Then the electric light bulb and battery which supplied the current for the door bell disappeared. Next the sound of a crash had everyone running to the kitchen, which was certainly empty of people. Under the gas oven was a broken saucer.

In the evening a medium who had been invited to help explain events suddenly called out, 'Look! That's going next!' And a brass bowl with a glass dish inside it fell to the floor. The glass broke into pieces and the brass bowl crumbled like a concertina.

'What a pity,' said one of Alma's friends as she picked up the bowl. 'You looked after that so well.'

And then, even as she spoke, the brass bowl straightened out, assuming its normal shape. There was not a trace of damage.

On and on went the mad parade of tricks. Inexplicable, at times childish, but always contrary to all the laws of science. Things do not simply occur in such a fashion, we tell ourselves. Yet at Beverstone Road they most certainly did. Who could explain how a mat could rise from the floor and wrap itself round the head of a policeman and later do the same to two Danish newspaper men? And how was it that a fender came crashing downstairs when there was no one upstairs? What about the vase, hurled by some unseen force?

Beverstone Road, Thornton Heath, scene of the poltergeist haunting. (Croydon Local Studies Library)

And what about the events in the early hours of Wednesday? Leslie and Alma, their lodger George Saunders and the reporter and a photographer who had agreed to stay the night were still not in bed at 2.30 am. They had stayed up, curious to know if there would be any other manifestations. Now, however, Alma thought that she would go to bed. Not surprisingly, she was tired. The events of the past few days had undoubtedly drained her.

No sooner had she gone upstairs than there was a series of violent thuds. The men rushed to the bottom of the staircase and Alma called down that she was all right and that the noise came from the back bedroom. When they went into the room they saw a heavy old-fashioned wardrobe lying across the bed, its full-length mirror shattered.

But before they could attend to the wardrobe there came a shout from the hallway. George Saunders lay sprawled there on his back. He was not hurt, he said, but he was winded; something, had barged into him and had deliberately pushed him down the stairs.

Allowing them no time to attend to Saunders, almost immediately there was another alarm. A chair from the back bedroom clattered down the stairs, hitting Alma, before coming to a halt in the hall. But its downward flight had been too fast to witness.

There was no other disorder that night and perhaps very little sleep for anyone. The spare room bed, incidentally, was dubbed the 'bed of ill omen' by the *Croydon Advertiser*, which reported, with some rearrangement of the facts, that its man, who had been intending to sleep in it, had narrowly escaped being crushed to death.

It was plainly obvious from the national coverage of the story that something quite out of the ordinary was occurring at the Fieldings' home. Nandor Fodor, chief research officer of the International Institute for Psychical Research, came to the house and never forgot his first visit. On that day he observed 29 unusual occurrences. He conceded that it would have been possible with a great deal of practice to contrive some of the manifestations but there were five occurrences which he could not ascribe to any normal cause. He saw the almost obligatory flying crockery; the saucer which simply left Alma Fielding's hand and then broke up in mid-flight; the cat's milk bowl which had been outside in the yard and which suddenly appeared in the kitchen, despite the fact that no one had opened the door. On and on went the smashing and the crashing. Yet remarkable though these events were and disastrous as they were to the household, the Fieldings remained remarkably cheerful and cooperative.

To the researchers it became clear that the focus of these astonishing happenings was Alma Fielding, for Donald had gone to stay with relatives and still matters had not settled down. And in any case, Fodor and his colleagues, Drs Wills and Evans, could see how Alma reacted when anything remarkable happened. It was as if she was in shock. Her heartbeat was fast, her pulse raised, and she trembled all over. She was invited to the Institute headquarters in Kensington for further investigation.

On Friday 25th February, Alma paid her first of many visits to the IIPR. Before the test began she was stripped and searched, and her handbag and everything loose was taken from her. Then she put on a simple gown with no pockets, provided by the Institute, and this she wore at all subsequent sessions. Almost as soon as she arrived a hair brush appeared in the seance room. She recognised it as her own. When she left home it had been on her dressing table.

Two research officers took Alma home by car. And in mid-journey there was yet another incident. A glove peeled itself off her hand – and disappeared. And then it reappeared and disappeared yet again. They stopped the car and while the two men held Alma's arms the glove still came and went.

At the Institute there was no doubt that this was a rare case, a gem of a case, dramatic in its excessive violence. Nine out of ten poltergeists involved adolescents but here was an adult at the centre of affairs. Fodor announced, 'It is a genuine and amazing case of the supernormal. There is certainly no fraud. We are satisfied there is something supernatural at work.' He and his colleagues expected that the phenomenon would last about four to six weeks.

In the last week of February, when the manifestations were lessening in frequency, the *Advertiser* man was still able to report seeing Alma one evening, researchers in attendance, with her arms stretched out before her and a comb in her hand. The comb disappeared. Then she put two pennies on the palm of her hand and predictably they disappeared. Next, seven disc-like imitations of coins were placed on her palms. Two went; then two more went. But the rest remained stubbornly where they were.

The following morning, the reporter was called to the Fieldings' bedroom. A large china pot which had been on the chest of drawers had moved from underneath some of Mr Fielding's clothes which were lying on it and had dropped onto the floor on the other side of the room. Though unremarkable compared with what had gone on during the week, it served as a reminder that the disturbances were not over.

Then at breakfast time, while Alma was pouring tea for the reporter, she suddenly paused, the tea-pot still in her hand. 'Put your hand in my pocket,' she told him. 'There's something there.' It was the comb which had disappeared the night before.

But now the manifestations, at least on the grand scale, had begun to subside. There were fewer breakages, although small articles were being increasingly moved from one room to another. The researchers were confident that the Fieldings were over the worst and paid them warm compliments on the way in which they had stood up to their ordeal, seeing practically all their glass and china destroyed and their heavy furniture damaged. This was the most violent poltergeist case that any of them had ever experienced and they were full of admiration for the Fieldings' fortitude.

Alma Fielding continued cooperating with the research, visiting the Institute twice a week. Whenever she was there, there was a rain of unexpected items. Saucers flew out of her hand, breaking in mid-air. And yet these were so strong that even the strongest man present could not break them with his hands. There were small boxes, fossils, pieces of pottery, coins and even white mice and a bird. She produced a spray of violet perfume that hung like a cloud that could be walked into and out of.

At times, Alma spoke of other previous strange experiences, of how, for example, in the previous year she had fallen into a trance and heard her father's spirit speak to her. When she became conscious again she found that a cross had been carved as with a knife on her breast. When she went to have it dressed, the doctor had discovered that there was a growth beneath the cross and was obliged to operate.

Then, during the research period, there was another astonishing occasion. On 19th June, Alma had been near The Old Fox public house at Coulsdon. She had had a vision of an evil-faced man which had frightened her terribly. Two days later, when Fodor put her into a trance, she revealed that the man had been hanged near the spot where she had had her vision. When she resumed consciousness she told Fodor and his colleagues that she could feel a tightening on her throat. As they watched, the researchers saw what appeared to be strangulation marks, two overlapping circles a quarter of an inch thick, biting into the flesh. It was just as if she had a noose around her neck. The observers had no doubt that there was no trickery involved.

There were many witnesses to the poltergeist outbreak at Beverstone Road. The professional researchers were convinced that it was genuine and emanating from some psychic disorder troubling Alma Fielding and that is where opinion stands on the matter today. And yet . . .

One day at the Institute a linen bag fell between Alma's ankles. She was wearing the robe she always wore during the research sessions. Where had the bag come from? Well, there are areas that cannot be searched without total embarrassment. For weeks, simply to keep matters going, it must be thought, simply because the ordinary suburban housewife wished to maintain her emergent celebrity status, Alma Fielding had carried on her person, inside the bag, small items such as coins, fossils, pins and the like. At appropriate moments she had contrived by powerful muscular effort and sleight of hand to release them. Perhaps a girl who had learnt to tight-rope walk when young, a girl whose mother was in a woman-sawn-in-half act, knew about certain show-business methods. Now Fodor was obliged by the Institute to withdraw from the research. Pity. For Alma Fielding, despite this later trickery, was an unusual case – witness the strangulation as well as the whole range of poltergeist pyrotechnics which drew attention to her.

Wonderful case. Quite remarkable. There were things at Beverstone Road which are almost beyond belief but that poltergeist activity on a grand scale occurred is undeniable. Sad that after it stopped Alma Fielding, seemingly desperate to hang on to her new-found fame, tried to use more mundane methods to prolong and sustain it.

THE RICHMOND BANK MURDER

It's a gold coloured Wolseley and it's 19 year old Sharon, his girl friend, who's driving. He's the passenger, sitting back, taking it easy. Not as if he hasn't been out and about already this morning, making the last-minute preparations for the job that he's so carefully planned. He needs the money. He's going away shortly, he knows that. They're going to send him down for years, no doubt about it. But when he comes out, when he's done his time, he'll have a nice little stash waiting if this job works out as it should. So this morning he's been out and bought a tin of boot polish. Boot polish, would you believe it? That'll fox them. That and the wig. They'll think it was a Pakistani who did it. Nice touch that. And he's had time this morning to saw off the shotgun barrels in his garage. Soon they'll be in Kingston. Park the car there. Drop Sharon. Get another car. Up to the bank and that's it.

As it turned out, Angela Woolliscroft met him only once. Even then it was only a brief meeting, lasting no more than a few seconds. Not many words were spoken. He had leaned against the safety glass, the gun barrel pointing at her, and had whispered to her urgently, his voice threatening, saying something like, 'Give me some money and hurry up about it.' Whether Angela made any reply is not known. But she was nowhere near the alarm and so she did as she was told, reaching into the drawer and sliding about £2,500 into the tray. She reached down again, presumably to find another bundle of notes, and it was then that he fired. The shot went right through the half-inch thick safety screen and Angela took the full brunt, falling backwards off her stool, the blood gushing from her face and throat.

He turned and walked out, dropping a yellow Marks & Spencer's mackintosh and a plastic bag on the way. He had no more need of them now, no need now for the stolen mac to hide the gun, no more need for the plastic bag which he had only minutes before picked up in the street, thinking it might be useful to carry his takings in. Calmly he walked over to the waiting car, a rather faded maroon Austin, and picked up a handful of mud from the gutter. He rubbed it over the registration plate and then drove off, leaving the 20 year old girl lying on the floor, failing to respond to the efforts of her shocked colleagues to save her.

Angela Woolliscroft from Chessington, employee at the Upper Ham Road branch of Barclays in Richmond for the past four years, had been anticipating with some excitement her trip to Jersey on the following day when she would represent the bank in a hockey tournament. But her life ended abruptly at 12.30 pm on Monday 10th November 1976. She was murdered in a brutal and casual manner by an unknown killer whose reckless attitude to human life, it would later be revealed, had been demonstrated on an earlier occasion.

But who was he? There was no sign of him. Detective Chief Superintendent Jim Sewell from Scotland Yard established an operations room in Richmond police station but there were no immediate suggestions about who might have committed this awful crime. There were no whispers from members of the underworld so many of whom draw the line at the ultimate violence, especially where someone so young, a girl so essentially decent, is concerned. Sewell, heading a team of 40 detectives, sent out appeals and ensured that the press, radio and TV kept the murder before the public. 'Someone knows this man had a gun,' he said, 'and someone knows about the stolen money.' But the statement produced no immediate concrete results. Nor indeed did Barclays' offer of a reward of £50,000, the highest ever for a bank raid in Britain.

There were some descriptions. A boy had seen the killer cross the road diagonally from his car very slowly and deliberately. He had noticed that. It seemed so odd to see someone in busy Upper Ham Road taking his time in that way at that time of day, a busy Monday lunchtime, when there was so much traffic about. He had also noticed that the man wore sunglasses.

Of the 11 bank staff only five had seen Angela's killer. The others had not noticed him walk either into or out of the bank. And those who had glimpsed him were not sure that they would

MURDER

ANGELA WOOLISCROFT, aged 20
WED 10 NOVEMBER, 12.30 pm

Barclays Bank, Upper Ham Road, Ham, Richmond
She was shot during a robbery in which £2,500 was stolen.

DID YOU SEE ANYTHING?
Please contact the Murder Squad at
RICHMOND POLICE STATION
Tel: 01·940 9595
All information treated as strictly confidential

The police appeal for witnesses, though the victim's surname was spelt incorrectly on the notice.

be able to identify him. But some salient features were recalled. His hair was long and black, his cheeks hollow and his complexion dark. Another witness who saw him go into the bank said something that must at the time have seemed rather odd. He thought the man had blackened his face.

This was a vast police operation. Sewell and his team were certain that they were not seeking some amateur criminal. This was a man who was both ruthless and capable of careful planning. How else could he have escaped in so casual a manner? An amateur would have been likely to panic at the enormity of what he had done. This man, whoever he might be, was a practised criminal: this man had walked calmly away from his murder and had effectively disappeared.

Over the following days and weeks the police chased thousands of leads. They raided houses, eliminating potential suspects from the crime, although in the course of their investigation they cleared up, almost incidentally, many other crimes. They interviewed 5,000 members of the public and made 15,000 house enquiries.

Miss Marshall, who lived in Mitcham, called the police to tell them that she had not bothered to report a minor theft from her car which she had left on the day of the murder in Bentalls' multi-storey car park in Kingston. She had thought her loss too insignificant. She had parked on the ninth floor and had not bothered to lock the car door. When she returned later in the day, she noticed that the car was not in the place where she had left it. She had assumed that car park staff had moved it. Perhaps, she thought, she had parked it in an inconvenient position. She had then noticed that her yellow Marks & Spencer's mac had gone and along with it her black sunglasses. She admitted that she had thought the theft too unimportant to bother with and anyway it was probably her own silly fault. And for some days she had not given it another thought. Not, that is, until she read that the Richmond bank murderer had been wearing black sunglasses and that he had dropped a yellow mac. And in addition, she told police, her car, an eight year old Austin A40, was maroon in colour.

It was clear that the killer had taken Miss Marshall's car to the bank. He had used her sunglasses as disguise and her mac to conceal his firearm. Then he had driven back to the car park, replacing the Austin in not quite the same place as he had found it. Presumably he had parked his own car in the multi-storey before the raid and had then picked it up again to drive away. Clever planning.

Now reports came in from members of the public who at about one o'clock on the day of Angela's death had been queueing up in their cars to enter the car park. The driver of an Austin A40 had forced his way through, hooting continuously and passing several of the waiting cars on the passenger side. Inevitably there had been heated words but the driver involved had not been deterred. Detective Chief Superintendent Sewell was in no doubt that this unidentified man was the bank killer.

But no one had seen him leave in a different car.

There was, however, a tip-off, one of many, which quite interested police. A man in Basingstoke had seen someone transfer what looked like a shotgun from one car to another. It transpired that this was Michael Hart, a 37 year old with a long criminal record for violence and theft. The police visited him. But he had an alibi. And anyway, he was on bail for his involvement in a jewel robbery and required to report twice a day to Basingstoke police station. How could he commit such a crime when he was

Michael Hart was quickly suspected of the killing.

under such restrictions? A search of his house produced nothing incriminating. In any case, at that stage, he did not quite fit the description of Angela Woolliscroft's murderer. Perhaps, police thought, it might be as well to keep him under observation for the time being and Basingstoke officers were detailed to look out for him just to ensure that he was not in some way involved.

The Basingstoke police were doubtless glad to watch out for Hart. He was suspected of 50 other robberies but in spite of strong police objections he had been allowed bail. Furthermore, the French police were requesting his extradition to face charges after a shoot-out near Charles de Gaulle airport only three months earlier. Hart had argued with a taxi driver over his fare and then attacked and stabbed him. When five policemen tried to arrest Hart, he had disarmed one of them and fired his pistol at the others several times. Fortunately he had missed. Then he had escaped. But Interpol had tracked him down. His lawyer, however, had asked local magistrates not to keep him in custody. His client had a fixed address, a family, substantial securities and he was willing to report to the police twice a day. So the police at Basingstoke, frustrated at his receiving bail, were not at all unwilling to keep an eye on him.

In the early hours of 23rd November, nearly a fortnight after the disastrous bank robbery, Hampshire police were called to an attempted robbery at a Basingstoke garage. Just as the police car arrived on the garage forecourt a blue Ford Cortina, its lights off, its tyres squealing, passed them at high speed, travelling in the opposite direction. There was a chase over several miles of country roads, the cars reaching speeds of up to 100 mph. Then the Cortina crashed. Out of the door on the driver's side lurched a man, making off over the fields. On such a pitch-black night, the officers had no chance of catching him. But they recognised Michael Hart. And although he did not surface for another month, his abandoned car contained material that was very interesting to the police.

In the car the police found, in addition to stolen jewellery, stolen driving licences and items of disguise, a French .22 Hendal automatic pistol and 72 rounds of ammunition.

Further enquiries about the pistol revealed that it had been stolen from a Reading gun dealer. On that occasion the thief had also taken a shotgun and several boxes of No. 7 Eley trap shot cartridges.

All of this was of great interest to Sewell and his officers. Clearly Michael Hart, whom they had felt merited observation but of whose responsibility for the Richmond bank raid they had had some doubt, ought now to be further questioned. If they could find him.

When the police went to his home in Basingstoke, Hart, unsurprisingly, was not there. His wife was but she was unable to tell them anything of his whereabouts. They showed her their search warrant. Under the stairs they found 19 shotgun cartridges stolen from the Reading gun dealer. And there was also a shotgun.

But if the police thought that their find pointed to Hart as the Richmond bank killer, their hopes were almost immediately dashed. The cartridges found in the motor car were labelled No. 7 trap shot whereas those which had killed Angela were No. 7 game shot. But Sewell was convinced now that Hart was the man they were seeking for the murder. He had the cartridges opened up and compared the shot in them with those taken out of Angela's body. They were identical.

Sewell then contacted the factory where the cartridges had been made. Would they look again at the trap shot cartridges which the police had found in the car? Back came the reply from the factory with an apology. There had been an almost unheard of computer error. The labelling system had gone awry. The cartridges were wrongly labelled as trap shot; they were really game shot. The search for Hart intensified. But where was he?

Sewell made an inspired guess. He knew that Hart was by trade a painter and decorator and he learnt that in August, between his various dishonest jobs, he had carried out some work at a petrol station belonging to a London garage chain. But he had not been paid. Sewell wondered if his suspect might shortly call at the firm's head office for his cash. The detective felt that now that Hart was on the run he might be desperate enough to present himself for payment. The staff at the office were warned that Hart might turn up and were asked to alert police if he came on the premises. And sure enough, on 20th January 1977, Hart appeared at the Hounslow office asking for his money. Within minutes he was arrested. He had for the past couple of months continued his life of crime, in the company of his girl friend, Sharon Stacey.

At Richmond police station, after his first interview, Hart was found attempting to hang himself from his cell door with his trouser belt. His breathing had already stopped but he was revived and over the next four days was interviewed on several occasions. He insisted time after time that he had not killed Angela Woolliscroft, that he had not raided the bank at Richmond.

Then, quite suddenly, in the presence of his wife and brother-in-law, he confessed that he had been at the bank and that his gun had shot Angela Woolliscroft. But, he said, it had been an accident.

He explained how on 10th November Sharon Stacey had driven him to Kingston and how he had taken Miss Marshall's Austin A40. He went on to tell how after the robbery he had returned to the car park with great difficulty as he had become snarled up in the unfamiliar one-way system. But eventually he picked up the Wolseley. Not that the return journey was trouble free. The car had broken down at Fleet and he had had to call on the RAC and take out membership of that association at the roadside. When he reached Basingstoke he went to the police station for his second reporting session of the day.

His disguise, the wig and the black boot polish on his face, had been, as he had hoped it would be, effective enough to prevent the police from recognising him from witnesses' descriptions.

Hart showed police where he had buried the sawn-off barrels of the shotgun in his garden. In one barrel there was a live cartridge, in the other a cartridge that had been fired. Both came from the incorrectly labelled batch. On his way home after the robbery, Hart said, he had thrown the shotgun into the Thames. He showed the police where it was and frogmen retrieved it. In its barrel was a spent cartridge of the wrongly labelled No. 7 game shot.

After the murder and robbery, Hart had been unable to return home and had stayed in a caravan with Sharon Stacey. At first Sharon admitted to police that she had driven Hart to Kingston on 10th November, saying that, tiring of waiting for him there, she had taken a train back to Basingstoke. Though she retracted her account, she was later to be given three years for crimes committed in the company of Hart.

Hart had claimed that the shooting of Angela Woolliscroft had been an accident. 'I told her to give me the money,' he told Sewell. 'She was ages and ages. I banged on the glass with the gun and told her to hurry up. The money dropped in the tray. It was then the gun went off.'

'I did not mean to use it,' he went on. 'I knew I had hit the girl because she screamed. I just hoped she was only wounded. I only found out she was dead when I heard about it on the TV.'

But forensic evidence suggested that there was no accident at the Richmond bank. Both barrels were already cocked when Hart walked into the bank. He was willing to admit that. His explanation was that the gun had responded to his tapping the barrels on the protective screen. Not true, according to the forensic experts, for to pull the trigger of the barrel that killed Angela needed six and a half pounds pressure. The trigger needed to be squeezed very firmly. And even when the gun's butt was dropped hard on the ground, it could not be made to fire. Only if it was dashed on a hard surface with such force that pieces of its wood chipped off would its trigger fire. No, it could not have been an accident.

There was further conclusive evidence that the gun retrieved from the river was the murder weapon. Lodged in the unfired barrel of the shotgun were a thousand tiny fragments of glass from the dead cashier's screen. Other pieces of this glass, incidentally, had been transferred from Hart's clothing to the stolen Austin car he drove immediately after the shooting.

Right to the end Michael Hart refused to admit that he had shot Angela Woolliscroft deliberately. But there was yet further evidence to support that allegation. Describing what had occurred, Hart said Angela bent over to collect money from the drawer on her right. As she straightened up, according to his version, the gun had discharged itself. But the forensic report showed that there was gunshot in her right hand. How could this be, the police asked, if as Hart had said she had been bending over to her right? Had she been bending in that direction, her right hand would have been below counter level. No, the police declared, the wounds she received were not the result of an accident. Hart knew what he was doing. Anxious to get the job done, he was perhaps irritated that she was not moving fast enough for him. A shot in rage? Or was it that he simply hoped to frighten her and others in the bank so that he could ensure a safe getaway? Yet everything points to Hart's being calm and collected throughout the robbery. Even after the girl fell off the stool, the blood spurting already from her neck and face, he seems not to have been unduly perturbed. And it has to be recalled that this is a man who had been involved in a shoot-out in Paris from which he had escaped

At his Old Bailey trial in November 1977, Hart still refused to acknowledge that he had murdered Angela Woolliscroft. He did however admit to over forty other offences.

The jury found him guilty of murder by a majority of eleven to one. Sentencing him to serve at least 25 years, Mr Justice Melford Stevenson described Michael Hart as a 'wicked and dangerous criminal'. And so he was.

If only he had not been granted bail. As it was, Michael Hart became the only man known to have committed a murder between fulfilling his bail obligations to report in the morning and evening to his local police station.

MYSTERY UPON MYSTERY

Railway tracks. They're not always the best places to be. Never know what you're going to find. And tunnels, well . . . But at least the men who carry out the maintenance are hardened. It takes a great deal to faze them. They encounter all sorts of unpleasantnesses in the course of their daily work. Even so, the sight they saw by torchlight in Merstham Tunnel late on Sunday 24th September 1905 was quite the worst that any of them ever had seen or ever would see.

The gang under their foreman, William Peacock, were just about to set to work about 400 yards from the south end of the mile-long tunnel on the London to Brighton line. It was there that they came across the severely mutilated body of a woman. At once

Merstham Tunnel where the dead woman was found.

Peacock went back to the railway station at Merstham, calling for a doctor and the police. Some hours later he sent a report to the London office. It read: 'Sub Inspector W. Peacock, while walking through Merstham Tunnel, at 10.55 this evening, found a female body about 400 yards from the end of the tunnel. The police took charge of the body and searched it. No address or ticket or money was found on it, and nothing to show who she was. The body is lying at the Feathers Hotel, awaiting an inquest.'

The body in the coach house of Merstham's Feathers Hotel was broken almost beyond recognition. The face was pulped, the nose smashed, the skull shattered, the top of the head sheared away at the hair line. The woman had worn a hat and part of the veil was embedded in the brain. Her left arm was crushed, her thighs broken and one leg almost detached.

Was this a suicide? Had the woman walked into the tunnel and thrown herself in front of a train? And who was she?

At first sight – only a guess was possible, given the extent of her injuries – she was in her mid-thirties, her hair still brown with not a sign of grey. Round her neck was a gold chain and locket, and she had several rings on her fingers. Obviously she was not a poor woman. She was well nourished and strongly built, and her hands bore no signs of manual work. Perhaps she was not obliged to have a job. Or possibly she might be a shop-girl or a clerk of some kind in an office. Her patent leather shoes were rather shabby and perhaps the fact that their owner had fitted circular rubber heels that could be revolved as they wore down indicated someone who was no fool with what money she had.

The dead woman wore a dress of black voile, flimsy, net-like. It was certainly not working dress. It was the kind of clothing a modest, respectable woman might wear for a social occasion.

Fortunately for those seeking to identify her, her underclothing carried laundry marks. These enabled her to be named within hours. On the Monday afternoon, she was identified by her brother Robert as Mary Sophia Money, aged only 22, who worked for Messrs Bridger and Co., dairymen, at 245 Lavender Hill, Clapham Junction.

If the first thoughts were that Sophia Money had walked into the tunnel seeking death, these were soon revised. Dr Henry Crickett, the local doctor who had been summoned to the tunnel, was of the view that she had fallen out or had been thrown out of the train travelling from London in the direction of Brighton. The doctor spotted on the sooty wall of the tunnel, at about 5 ft 8 ins from the ground, horizontal markings stretching about 40 feet. In his opinion these indicated where her head and hands had hit the tunnel wall. From here, he said, she had rebounded onto the line and under the wheels either of the train on which she had been travelling or of a train coming along later. She had died instantaneously. He also reported that when he arrived the body was still warm and that therefore she must have died only an hour or so earlier.

But a suicide? Well, half a dozen years later that was still being postulated as the manner in which Mary Sophia Money met her death. But it was neverthless difficult to accept. Even the Coroner's open verdict seems rather indecisive.

For in Sophia's mouth there was a gag. She had left home wearing a white silk scarf and this was so deeply thrust into her mouth that the police had difficulty in removing it. Inside the mouth, to the gums, the roof and the tongue, the doctor noticed abrasions and bruises. He believed that these were the result of the scarf being forced into her mouth by someone's fingers or – can it possibly be credited? – 'possibly the end of a stick'. And were some of the bruises on the body sustained in a struggle in the compartment? Was this where the young woman lost two of her teeth?

Speaking to a reporter, Dr Crickett explained that Sophia had not been suffocated by the gag. He thought that right to the end she was struggling with her assailant 'and that she was thrown out, still alive, by a person of some strength'.

So a murder? Any other helpful clues? Very few. Save that Sophia had left home with her purse which contained her week's wages. And now there was no sign of the purse in the tunnel or along the line nor in any of the carriages in any of the trains that she might have travelled in. Had Sophia Money suffered her awful end simply for a week's wages?

The police endeavoured to discover if anything of significance had happened in Sophia's last hours. What extraordinary event had occurred which led to her death? But none was ever found. The day of her death, a Sunday, seems to have been no more remarkable than any other. There was nothing of note. There was simply a gap in time which the detectives working on the case were never able to resolve satisfactorily.

Sophia lived at the dairy in Lavender Hill where she worked. On the day on which she died she was on duty, as she was every fourth Sunday, from one o'clock until seven. Working with her was another girl, Emma Hone, who was able to fill in some details of the day. Emma said that although Sophia was very reserved she was a good-natured girl. On Sundays she often would stay in the house writing letters and if she did go out, as she sometimes did to visit friends living in Victoria, she was usually home by half past ten.

On the Sunday in question, Sophia announced that she was going out for 'a little walk', telling Emma that she would not be late. It does seem remarkable that she did not so much as hint at where she was going. Nor did she mention that she intended to meet anyone. Perhaps Emma was not too surprised at Sophia's reticence. She seems to have been accustomed to this very private girl. But Emma and she parted on good terms. Sophia, she said, was her usual cheerful self.

Did the fact that Sophia did not take a jacket with her suggest that she had gone out for only a short time? Had she intended to stay out late, might she not have thought that she ought to take it to ward off the chill of a late September night? Mere speculation, of course. The young do not always consider such matters important.

When she left the house Emma saw that Sophia was carrying her black cotton purse. She thought that it probably contained a substantial amount of money. Sophia had received her wages earlier in the day and when the police searched her belongings they found no sign of any cash. They assumed that she had taken her money with her. But there was no sign of the purse or cash at the site of her death.

The house at Lavender Hill was always locked up for the night at 11 o'clock and Sophia was most often home by then. On this occasion, however, she was not and consequently, Emma waited to let her in. It can be assumed that this was a mutual arrangement between the two girls. When, however, she had not returned by one o'clock, Emma assumed that she was staying the night with friends and went to bed.

That was as much as the police could learn from Emma Hone. But there was another witness. Frances Golding kept a sweet shop in Station Approach, only a short distance from where Sophia lived in Lavender Hill. She knew Sophia as a fairly regular customer, who often called in on Wednesdays and Sundays.

Sophia had paid her usual visit at about seven o'clock, just minutes after she had left Emma Hone. She had bought six penn'orth of chocolate, taking her money out of the black purse, and had stayed in the shop for more than five minutes, chatting cheerfully if inconsequentially and principally about sweets. Interesting, this chat, in its lack of any real substance. Nothing about what she had been up to in recent days. No indication of any exciting plans. Nothing personal at all. Nothing except that she was going to catch a train up to Victoria. And then what? She did not go into that, Frances Golding said. And perhaps she would have been surprised if she had, for that was not Sophia's way, though she was a most bright and amiable girl.

And what about young men, Miss Golding was asked. Had Sophia ever mentioned a young man? Never.

But mention of this proposed trip to Victoria is worth considering. Only minutes before, Emma had been told that Sophia was intending to take 'a little walk'. Now, Victoria is no great distance from Clapham but it is not 'a little walk'. It is only a short train ride, most certainly, but a short train ride cannot be described as a little walk. So, had Sophia changed her plan after leaving the house? Or was there some reason for not explaining fully to Emma Hone what her plans for the evening were?

When Sophia walked out of the sweet shop in Station Approach she went to Clapham Junction railway station. A couple of days later a ticket collector at the station recognized her from a photograph. She had been on her way to Victoria, he said, though whether he actually saw her ticket or whether she simply said the name of the station as she passed through is not clear from the evidence.

So here is Sophia, smartly dressed, and presumably on her way to Victoria. To do what? Is she conducting an affair? It later transpires that she has a young man with whom she walks out on Wednesdays. But he lives in Harrow and he has a cast-iron alibi for the Sunday. But then, who says that young, attractive women may not meet other young men? Was Sophia also meeting a second suitor?

And from now, there are only sightings of women who might or might not be Sophia. But it is not even certain which train she was on. The assumption from the evidence given by Dr Crickett is that she died at about ten o'clock at night. She might therefore have caught a train which left London Bridge at 9.33 pm and passed through the tunnel at 9.55 pm. Alternatively, she could have been on the train which left Charing Cross at 9.33 pm and passed through the tunnel at about 10.05 pm.

So who was the young woman seen by the guard on the train from London Bridge when he opened the door of a first-class carriage for one of the boarding passengers at East Croydon? It so happened that the passenger saw that the carriage was already occupied and decided to move on to an empty compartment. The young, plump-faced woman was wearing a dark dress, just as Sophia had been. And round her neck she wore, according to the guard, 'a long muslin looking thing'. Sophia had been savagely gagged by a scarf. Sitting next to her was a tallish, powerfully built man with 'a long face and thin chin'.

At the next stop the guard glanced in the carriage again. The couple were still there on the far side of the compartment. The arm rest had been pulled up. The guard thought their movements were suspicious. He had the idea that they were trying to avoid being seen. Sophia and her mystery lover? Or merely a couple seeking the partial privacy of a first-class carriage, safe enough in those days of non-corridor trains from prying eyes when the train was in motion. Were they simply embarrassed to have the guard peering in each time they came to a stop?

At Redhill, the guard saw that the door to the compartment was open. A man walking towards the exit looked not unlike the man he had seen in the carriage. But he was alone. Where was the girl? Or was he mistaken? Had the man and his lady friend left the train earlier? In any event, this testimony was quite useless as was that of the signalman at Purley Oaks, north of Merstham. He thought he saw a couple struggling in a first class carriage of this same train as it passed his box. But such evidence was too vague to help the police in their enquiries.

There was of course a full-scale investigation, mainly focusing on Sophia's boyfriends. Robert Money, Sophia's brother, had told the Coroner: 'She knew several young fellows. In fact they have run after her.' He then named two men, one who lived in Harrow, whom she met every Wednesday night, and another, whose home was in Brentford but both of these were eliminated from police enquiries.

It was Robert Money who in the weeks following her death offered other possible names to the investigating officers. At one time there was a suggestion that the police were poised to make an arrest, but the gaggle of newspaper men who made their way to Molesey were disappointed. No one was arrested.

At Robert's instigation another man, Charles Bellchambers, was questioned. He had been a friend of the girl and had in fact given her a ring the previous year but on the night in question he was miles away in Berkhamsted and could prove it. Sophia's employer, Arthur Bridger, was also closely questioned about his relationship with her. He denied ever having given her presents, but there was some suggsetion that he had been seen with her at Bognor. But even that did not place him in a railway carriage on the fateful Sunday night.

Eventually the police were to become somewhat irritated by Robert's suggestions and even some contradictory statements which at times set them running off in all directions. He told them that it was unlikely that Sophia would have gone to meet a man on that Sunday evening. Certainly, he said, she would not have allowed a stranger to trick her into going with him onto a train which was taking her away from home. She was, he said, 'a most nervous girl who always shrank from male society'. And this is plainly incorrect. Sophia Money was quite at ease in the company of men. She was a business-like young woman, who, when her mother died, had handled the sale of the family dairy.

In 1908, when all interest in the case seemed to have died down, there was another sudden spurt of police interest. They had of course by then persuaded themselves that this was a case of suicide, allowing themselves to forget the gag in Sophia's mouth. When one Albert Cooper wrote to the police naming his friend William Wakeman as the murderer, they followed up the accusation. The day before Sophia died, Cooper recalled that he had tried to borrow Wakeman's walking stick, presumably regarded as a fashion item. Wakeman had refused, saying that he was going to meet 'a very special tart' and implying that he needed to impress her with his appearance. After the murder, Cooper recalled, his friend had some minor scratches and bruises and kept to his basement for several days, coming out only after dark. More recently the two men had quarrelled and Cooper had said, 'I know something which could hang you.' William Wakeman had turned pale at the threat. Unsurprisingly nothing came of this daft tale.

So the dreadful death of Sophia Money remains a mystery. It seems not unreasonable to speculate that it was she whom the guard and even the signalman at Purley Oaks saw in the carriage. Had she had an assignation that night? Did she and her male companion decide to ride in the comparative seclusion of a first-class compartment? And then was there a dispute as the man overstepped the bounds?

Or here is an interesting little event which may or may not have some link with Sophia's death. In August 1912, almost six years later, a man called Robert Hicks Murray took a house in Enys Road in Eastbourne. One morning the fire brigade was called to the house. It was an inferno. When finally the firemen gained access they found five bodies. Murray had shot his wife, his three children and himself. Another woman, who turned out to be not only Murray's sister-in-law but his bigamous wife, was injured.

Murray had brought them down from Clapham, ostensibly for a holiday. Instead he was inviting them to be murdered. Life had proved too much for him. His world was based on a rotten structure of fantasy. He claimed to be a military man with connections in Scotland. Even his two wives were uncertain where the truth began and where it ended. For a considerable time neither was aware that he was maintaining the other. He kept two separate homes going.

Nor was he 'Captain' Murray. Nor had he seen service in the Gordon Highlanders or the Scots Guards. He was just plain Robert Money, fantasist. And sometimes he was Captain McKay or Captain Stirling.

And he was the brother of Sophia Money.

Until shortly after her death he had been a dairyman. Then came a life change. Chief Inspector Fox at Scotland Yard took part in the investigation into Sophia's death and he had several conversations with Robert Money. He regarded his attitude as satisfactory and said that he did all that a brother might be expected to do in the circumstances, no more and no less. But six months after her death, Fox again met Money and was struck by the sudden change in both his manner and appearance since they had last met. Still jocular and well spoken, he now looked less like a dairyman and more like a man about town.

In 1906 Robert Money had sold his share in a dairy business

and used the capital to build six houses in Hampden Road, Norbiton. He rented these out and seemed to have, according to his surviving wife, 'abundant money'. Then, in the months before the Enys Road murders, he sold up all the houses. Was there a sudden financial problem? He earned £2.14s each week from rents but he had two families to keep. Why the odd facade, the assumption of false identities, the bigamous marriage involving sisters?

Did this have anything to do with his sister's death years earlier? Did this fatally unbalanced man murder his sister?

In 1912 the police inevitably had to reconsider Robert's 1905 alibi but were unable to shake it. They continued in the belief that Sophia had committed suicide by jumping from a train. Ex-Superintendent James Brice of the Surrey Constabulary now felt he ought to release information that had been held back at the time of the 1905 investigation when it was believed that its publication would upset other family members. He said, 'She gambled extensively. Her stock at the dairy shop in which she was an assistant was short, and she feared being found out.' This, the police believed, drove her to suicide.

But the terrible mystery of Sophia Money has never been resolved. All sorts of possibilities come to mind. The reader will understand what these are.

THE HAUNTING OF ASH MANOR HOUSE

Ash Manor House at Ash Green was the scene of the most exciting ghost-laying experiments for years. In 1934 the 13th century house, secluded and set in 24 acres of woodland, had been purchased by an American family, the Kellys, recorded in accounts written shortly after the dramatic events under the pseudonym Keel. Maurice Kelly and his wife Kathleen, an outstandingly beautiful woman, lived at the manor with their 16 year old daughter Gladys. A bedroom in the house, occupied by the butler and his wife, was allegedly haunted but for the past 20 years there had been no reports of any supernatural disturbances.

The Kellys' first awareness of anything untoward was when they heard what sounded like footsteps in the attic. Impossible, they thought; there were no longer any floorboards up there for anyone to walk on. Then one night in November 1934 when they had been in occupation for five months, Maurice Kelly was roused at three in the morning by three violent bangs on his bedroom door. He ignored them, just as he ignored the two bangs at the same hour the next night and the single bang on the third night. The next three nights he was away from home on business, but on the first night of his return he was again disturbed by a fierce banging on the door at three in the morning. As he struggled to awaken he was aware that there was someone else in the room. There, just beyond the bed, he saw a short figure. A tramp, was Kelly's first thought, for he was no believer in ghosts. Climbing out of bed, he made a thrust towards the oddly dressed intruder. But the stranger was elusive and somehow evaded his grip. Kelly made another dart at the man but this time his hands went right through the body before him. Terrified, he ran out of the bedroom and across the passageway and into his wife's bedroom, where he fainted. And as Kathleen Kelly got out of her bed, she too saw the bent-up figure of the little old man wearing old-fashioned clothes: a green smock, a pudding basin hat and muddy leggings. She did precisely what her husband had done. She aimed a blow at the stranger who had dared to invade her house but only succeeded in bruising her hand on the doorpost.

Over the next two years the Kellys saw the apparition on several occasions and usually at three in the morning. At times he would emerge from behind the chimney breast on the landing. On some occasions they would see him walk into a cupboard that had at one time marked the doorway of a priest's hole. Other times they would see him in the passage. They disliked the visitor. 'His face was very red, the eyes malevolent, the mouth open and dribbling,' Katherine said. Oddly, she was able to make him disappear simply by reaching out to touch him.

And there was the time when he looked straight at Mrs Kelly; as he raised his head, she saw for the first time the great gash in his neck, its flesh brutally torn and the gristly windpipe sticking out. And how was it that they could hear the apparition's footsteps as he walked over the carpeted floor or upstairs over the unboarded attic floor? Increasingly desperate about their situation and conscious of a sense of evil, they called in an exorcist without success. Eventually they contacted Dr Nandor Fodor, a psychoanalyst, at that time research officer for the International Institute for Psychical Research. It was he who persuaded Eileen Garrett, an internationally celebrated medium, to investigate what was happening at Ash Manor. It turned out to be one of the most intriguing cases in which she was involved.

The first visit was to prove astonishing. After being introduced to the Kellys, Mrs Garrett went into a trance and her spirit control, Uvani, described by Fodor as 'a kind of manager from the other side of life', then took over, speaking through her. He told the listeners, the Kellys, Fodor and Dr Elmer Lindsay, an American psychoanalyst, that he sensed a great unhappiness in the house. It was just the sort of place for an unhappy spirit to be attracted to. 'Haven't you discovered,' he asked, presumably addressing himself to Maurice and Kathleen Kelly, 'that these things happen to you when you are in a bad emotional state, physically or mentally disturbed? Don't you realise that you yourself vivify this memory?'

SURREY

Near Ash Green Station, ¾ mile from Ash Junction, 6 miles from Guildford.

In a delightful unspoiled District, Close to the Hog's Back, Within Daily Reach of London.

Illustrated Particulars, Plan and Conditions of Sale of the

FREEHOLD HISTORICAL
XIIIth CENTURY RESIDENCE

Ash Manor House
Ash Green

Of medium size, in excellent order throughout and

Carefully Restored and Modernised yet Retaining all its Old World Atmosphere and Charm.

Electric Light.   *Co.'s Water.*   *Main Gas and Electric Light available.*

Wealth of Old Oak and Characteristic Features.

PICTURESQUE OAST HOUSE affording Stabling and Garage, etc.

PRETTY INEXPENSIVE GARDENS

with Tennis Lawn, Stream, Kitchen Garden, and Well-timbered Pasture.

Standing in centre of

ABOUT 24 ACRES

thus ensuring seclusion.

TO BE SOLD BY AUCTION

as a Whole or in Four Lots at the

London Auction Mart, 155, Queen Victoria Street, E.C.4

On TUESDAY, 5th JUNE, 1934

At 2.30 p.m. precisely (unless previously sold privately).

Illustrated Particulars, Plan & Conditions of Sale may be obtained of Messrs. RICHARDS, BUTLER, STOKES & WOODHAM SMITH, Solicitors, Cunard House, Leadenhall Street, London, E.C.3 ; or of

Messrs. Geo. Trollope & Sons

Estate Agents, Surveyors & Auctioneers,

*25, Mount Street, Grosvenor Square, W.1;   5, West Halkin Street, Belgrave Square, S.W.1;
13, Hobart Place, Eaton Square, S.W.1;   45, Parliament Street, Westminster, S.W.1.
* Telephone: Grosvenor 1553 (3 lines).*

71. Sale of Ash Manor House, June 1934

The sale notice that led to the Kellys purchasing the property in 1934.

In other words, he was saying the intensely deep tensions between the members of the household attracted another deeply disturbed spirit. It was their emotional upheavals which produced the ghost of the old man. They in effect were encouraging him to manifest himself, constructing him out of their own personal distress. What they now needed to do, Uvani said, was to raise the ghost and then persuade him to leave.

Uvani then spoke of an old gaol which in the 15th century had existed about 500 yards to the west of the house. It seems not to have been for common criminals but for temporary prisoners of state. Or for those who displeased the local nobility. Over the years dozens had died in this gaol and Uvani spoke of their unhappy spirits which were still in the neighbourhood. This, he said, explained the presence here of the old man. 'If a particular spirit comes to trouble you, it is because he has an affinity with you.' A sense of old tragedies with which the house and its members had been associated had occupied the Kellys' unconscious minds.

At this point Uvani withdrew, leaving Mrs Garrett still in a trance-like state but now she began to alter. Her face, usually so maternal, seemed to alter, to take on the cast of an old man's. The cheeks appeared sunken, her mouth agonised, her whole expression tortured. Eileen Garrett was possessed.

Mrs Kelly stood up and looked closer at the medium.

'My God,' she said, her voice breathy with fear. 'It is the image of the ghost.'

Mrs Garrett raised both hands to her mouth. She tapped her fingers on her lips. It was as if a dumb man sat in the chair.

Then with hesitant fingers Mrs Garrett explored the skin of her neck and the Kellys recalled the awful gashed throat, the windpipe exposed. She raised her hand, indicating to Fodor that he should come forward to her chair. And then, when Fodor stood before her, she threw herself onto her knees before him, at the same time seizing his hand with a grip so powerful that he was in excruciating pain. It was as if the hand that held him wore a mailed glove. Fodor, afraid his hand would be broken, called out to Lindsay to help release him, but despite their joint efforts there was no freeing him. For two days afterwards Fodor's hand was bruised and sore.

And then, a strangled voice came from Mrs Garrett. The ghost could speak.

'Eleison! Eleison!'

'Lord have mercy,' he was saying, using words from the Roman Catholic mass.

Was he asking Fodor for mercy? Did he take him for his gaoler?

Fodor, his hand still in the relentless grip, called out that he was with friends. They had come not to do him harm but to help him. He must trust in them. Over and over, Fodor and Lindsay urged him that he must have faith in them, that he need have no fear of them.

And then, out of Mrs Garrett's throat, a story unfolded. It was strangely told, in a croaking voice, hesitant, full of unaccustomed words and fierce, angry denunciations.

He had been betrayed, he said. The Earl of Huntingdon had betrayed him. So had the Duke of Buckingham. Which Huntingdon? Which Buckingham? The narrative was never clear on that.

Though some accounts say that the ghost was a son of Lord Henley, the words that Fodor recorded in shorthand at this sitting indicate instead that his father was a liegeman, a subject, of that lord. The ghost explained how Buckingham had offered him money and land in return for Dorothy, his wife. When he had

Ash Manor as it looked when the Kellys moved in.

refused to cooperate, Buckingham had cast him into the gaol adjacent to Ash Manor House and separated him from his son. Out of Mrs Garrett's mouth came the strangulated curse: 'May his soul burn for ever in that hell from which there can be no escape.'

His name, he told Fodor, was Charles Edward but no family name was offered. He had a son, John Edward Charles, who was 'fighting, even now, for his ungrateful king'. And the king too had somehow played his part in the betrayal. But which king was never revealed.

Now the ghost, still speaking through Mrs Garrett, asked for a quill pen. Fodor handed him a pencil and a note pad. In strange characters, the pencil in the medium's hand, wrote 'Henley . . . Edward . . . Charles . . . Lord Huntingdon . . . Earl Huntingdon . . . Esse.'

'Esse', the medieval name of Ash village.

Then came more cryptic comments. Buckingham, once a childhood friend of Charles Edward, had taken Dorothy, and 'forced her eyes'. Did this mean that he had blinded her? Or did 'forced her eyes' mean that Buckingham had seduced her?

Now Charles Edward begged Fodor not to leave him. He knew he was a friend, that he intended him no harm. 'Do not leave me,' he implored, 'but help me to attain my vengeance.'

It was all too late, Fodor told him. All that he spoke of was long in the past. And anyway, matters of vengeance should be left to God.

'You prate to me of God?' Charles Edward replied angrily. 'He let me suffer. I want my vengeance.'

Now Lindsay and Fodor tried to persuade the tortured soul to trust them. He should give up his idea of revenge.

Could he not understand, they asked him. 'You are dead,' they explained. 'Centuries have passed since you were murdered. What do you want? Vengeance? Or do you want to join your wife and son?'

At first the ghost feared that his wife would not wish to see his poor tortured body but finally, after a struggle, Charles Edward seemed to accept what he was being told, to realise his position, to recognise that he was dead.

Suddenly, the spirit reached out to hold Fodor's hand again, calling out: 'Hold me! Hold me! I cannot stay. I am slipping. Don't leave me! Don't leave me!'

But now the grip relaxed, the voice silenced and Mrs Garrett, exhausted, lay back in her chair.

Had they released the unhappy spirit of a man murdered centuries past? Had they set him free?

It was the Kellys who were dubious about what they had witnessed. Fodor had told Charles Edward that he should now go off to meet his wife and son. But what if he failed to meet them, the Kellys asked. What then? Had they, Fodor and Lindsay, not promised the anguished spirit too much?

The next day, somewhat scornfully, Maurice Kelly phoned Fodor. The apparition had returned. 'He is standing in the doorway, trying to open his mouth to speak,' Kelly told him.

Immediately Fodor went across to Eileen Garrett's house in Kensington to arrange another consultation with Uvani. When he arrived, Dr Lindsay was already there with an odd story to tell him. Earlier that day Lindsay had been to the British College of Psychic Science, where he had been working with another psychic, Mrs Ruth Vaughn. She knew nothing of the events of Ash Manor, but when she went into a trance it appeared that her spirit control knew what had been happening there. As Lindsay had watched, Mrs Vaughn's hand had strayed to her mouth. He recognised the movements of the fingers, the tapping of the lips. He recalled Eileen Garrett in the chair at Ash Manor. Then Mrs Vaughn had leaned towards him, trying to grasp his hand and shouting in a terrified voice, 'None of this! I did not call you! I did not want you!'

Now the spirit confided in Lindsay how disappointed he had been. He had seen his son but not his wife. Where was she? He had gone to Ash Manor the previous night but Fodor and Lindsay, after all their promises to help, were not there. They too had betrayed him.

After Lindsay had finished his account of this curious possession of Mrs Vaughn, Mrs Garrett went once more into a trance. Uvani explained that Charles Edward was confused and in need of further assistance. The Kellys, according to Uvani, had not really cooperated. At first they had been interested but when the ghost had come to life they had been shocked and now they did not wish him to be released. 'They have used this poor, unhappy creature over a period of months to embarrass each other,' Uvani said. 'If they continue to supply the atmosphere that they do at present, they will make the house haunted and unhappy for future tenants.'

Fodor sent a transcript of this seance to the Kellys. How would they respond to such a bizarre accusation that they were hindering the release of the ghost? Somehow their emotional need for him seemed to keep their marriage going.

In a phone call to Fodor next day, Maurice Kelly confessed the truth of the matter. He and his wife were aware that the ghost manifested himself at a time of domestic tension. He admitted that there was serious emotional warfare in the house and that the ghost presumably had responded to this, recognising his own desperate unhappiness in others. This acknowledgement of their responsibilty for raising the ghost effectively laid it to rest. Thereafter, no more was heard of Charles Edward at Ash Manor House.

Could it really be the ghost which held the Kellys' marriage together? Were there centuries of emotional disturbance here in this old house? Had the profound unhappinesses of the nearby gaol in some way seeped into the very walls of the place, affecting its atmosphere, making it too a desperately unhappy place? And had the arrival of the Kellys, with their disturbed emotional baggage, raised the ghost? For there was emotional turmoil, unspeakable tensions. Maurice Kelly's homosexuality distressed his sex-deprived wife; her serious addiction to drugs disturbed him; their daughter's father-fixation combined with her jealousy of her mother affected the whole household. Here then, Fodor concluded, in this combination of old and new miseries, was the source of the psychic disturbances at Ash Manor House.

Nevertheless, there are still some curiosities in this bizarre ghost tale. Thirty years later Nandor Fodor was still unable to explain the matter totally satisfactorily. Researchers were still unable to work out the identity of the ghost. Historians had been unable to unravel the story of Buckingham, Huntingdon and Henley. Language experts had not been absolutely convinced of the authenticity of the ghost's speech and writing. Others queried the name Charles Edward, which was quite unmedieval. Lt Col. Mansfield, a handwriting expert, accepted that the writing on Fodor's pad was not Eileen Garrett's natural hand. Indeed, in his view after extensive tests, she was incapable of reproducing the script that the spirit had produced through her. He made her copy the name 'Henley' for five hours until she could reproduce it accurately but even then with the slightest disturbance she reverted to her own hand.

Mrs Eileen Garrett was a well-respected, highly reliable medium, who experienced observers were convinced had been possessed by Charles Edward. Dr Nandor Fodor was a scholar and a genuine and knowledgeable student of the paranormal, whose hand had been damaged by a ghost. The Kellys were in no doubt that they had seen an apparition and had recognised it when Mrs Garrett was possessed by the spirit.

Odd case, really, especially as the spirit control, Uvani, had divined the reasons for the psychic disturbances at Ash Manor House. He, a spirit, had psychoanalysed two minds and the ghost they had conjured up. Odd, indeed.

Just a Couple of Pocket Cowboys

It was not until the early morning of the Wednesday that Mandy the police dog alerted her handler, Sergeant Keith Simmonds, to the body. It had been covered with bracken but the dog nosed it out.

The dead man, lying face down, had been tied up round his ankles, thighs and midriff with a heavy-duty adhesive tape of a quite distinctive yellow and green. Round his neck were yards of rope and more tape. He had been gagged with his own tie. And then he had been shot in the back of the head, three times, with a small calibre, low velocity weapon fired at close range.

Now began the massive man-hunt for whoever had committed this awful crime, which looked so much like a gang slaying. But the police knew enough about the victim to make that hugely unlikely. Might it be a terrorist execution? Or poachers? But do poachers go to such extreme lengths? Would they have tied up someone so elaborately?

A 58 year old amateur ornithologist, a keen photographer, a member of Surrey Archery Society, John George just did not fit the bill of someone involved with gangland. After all, engineers employed by the Thames Water Authority were not the expected targets of hitmen. Nor were they the type to be the choice of terrorists. And the idea of poachers was instantly dismissed.

John George was said to be a quiet, law-abiding man with an enthusiasm for the countryside. And the more the police delved into his life the more confirmation they received from colleagues and friends that he was 'hard working and decent', that he was a 'shy man', 'a damn nice man', 'an inoffensive chap' and 'a nervous, intellectual type of man'.

So who could have wanted to murder this essentially decent

man in so brutal and so unexpected a fashion. Who? And why? For the motive was not apparent.

This wretched story unfolded at Dunsfold, that delightful south Surrey village, an exquisite little place with a wonderful 13th century church and fine old houses and cottages. Quiet and tranquil, Dunsfold, a quintessential English village, set amid woods and meadows, seems far away from the ills of the world. It is a place for restoring battered spirits, for soothing bruised hearts.

The tale began in the early afternoon of Tuesday 24th April 1979, when three men were seen to walk into a copse on the outskirts of the village, just off the A281 road to Bramley. They had parked their cars, a white Citroen estate and a blue Renault 20, in the narrow road just on the edge of the woodland. Two of them were carrying long-barrelled guns, one with a large ammunition magazine. But this did not surprise either of the Water Board men working down the lane. After all, this was the Godwin-Austen estate. It was woodland stocked with pheasant and deer. Every month local rough shooters visited these woods with shotguns to enjoy a spot of shooting. All part of conservation, all devoted to keeping the woodland's population in balance.

Within minutes shots were heard and they occasioned no surprise. But shortly afterwards two men ran out in what seemed to be a panic. So odd was their behaviour, so strange that now, apparently no longer a threesome, they should race to their cars in such a fashion. Were they deer poachers? One of the men climbed into the Citroen and the other into the Renault, not pausing to settle themselves but roaring their engines, ready to race off. Certainly the workmen sensed that there was something amiss and they were determined not to allow deer poachers off the hook so easily. Had these men shot an animal and callously left it wounded? They ran to their own van and tried to block the exit of the two cars. But it was too late. The drivers raced at them and then both in turn mounted the verge and skilfully manoeuvred their way round and onto the main road, making for Bramley. But something was clearly wrong, of that the Water Board men were convinced, and so was the local who joined them. He had been walking down the lane when the two cars flashed past him. Driven by two young men, he said. He'd taken the car registration numbers, he told the Water Board men. They agreed that he ought to pass on his information to the police.

It was not until later that night that Phyllis George reported her husband missing. He had driven to work at Godalming as usual, she said, but he had not returned to his home. She described her husband; she described the car, a blue Renault. And then the search started. Police began to link John George's disappearance with the odd business at Dunsfold which had been reported to them. And then, in the early morning of Wednesday, just about the time when George's body was found, came an interesting lead. Just after midnight, at Cadnam in the New Forest, two masked men entered a restaurant after the last of the customers had left, and held the proprietor and his family at gunpoint. The men had taken cash and had driven off in a blue Renault.

The people in this incident reported that one of the men carried what they described as a sub-machine gun. This tallied with eye-witnesses at Dunsfold, who had noted that one of the men carried a weapon with a long magazine.

Could these be the two men who had run out of the woodland at Dunsfold? And were they the smartly dressed, well-spoken pair of masked men who, according to reports from Kent police, on the preceding Saturday at 3.30 am had forced their way into the Coombe House restaurant at Hoo St Mary, near Rochester? These men apparently had a meal in the restaurant, presumably assessing the situation, and had waited in the car park in a white Citroen until only the head waiter and one waitress were on the premises. They had carried shotguns and had taken £300 from the safe. They had, their victims claimed, been considerate. They had offered the waitress a cardigan, as she was cold, and poured the head waiter a Scotch and had given him cigarettes. Before locking their captives in the wine cellar, the robbers had promised to telephone the police after an hour so that they would be released. This promise was kept.

While police were drafted in from all over the county to make a minute search of the Dunsfold murder site, a countrywide operation was launched to find the murderers. The police were in no doubt that they were the Cadnam restaurant robbers who had arrived and left in John George's Renault. Detective Chief Superintendent Ron Underwood, head of Surrey CID, announced that were looking for a blue Renault with a roof rack and at the same time were searching for a man who they thought might help them to identify the white Citroen.

By the Wednesday evening, road blocks were set up at Beckington, near Frome in Somerset. Residents of the village were told to stay indoors but no explanation was immediately given. But the police had now checked car registration numbers and knew that the owner of the Citroen was 22 year old John Nicholas Gerald Richards, who had changed his name by deed poll to Nicholas Manikum. He had relatives, absolutely respectable people, living in Beckington. When questioned, they had no idea where Nicholas was.

And the second man? This was 20 year old Jason Neil Andrew Richards, brother of Nicholas. Earlier in the year the two men had travelled to England from their home in Minorca. Their names and photographs were now released and published in the newspapers. Nicholas was wanted for murder and Jason for questioning. For a day or two the young men, described as antique dealers, seemed to have completely disappeared. Further enquiries centred around Bournemouth and Wimborne but these produced nothing. Some police officers flew to Minorca but there was no sign of their quarry there. Interpol was also sent details for general distribution throughout Europe.

Then there was a breakthrough in the hunt for the two men. The white Citroen estate, last seen at the murder spot, was found abandoned in Guernsey. The brothers had arrived there on Thursday 26th April. They had travelled by ferry from Weymouth under the name Manikum.

Early on Friday a 42 ft luxury motor-yacht, *Memet*, was reported missing from the harbour at St Peter Port. It had been taken during the night. Coastguards and shipping were immediately alerted and asked to be on the lookout. There was little doubt that the brothers were aboard. Nicholas had enough nautical skill and confidence to manage the craft. Police guessed that he and his brother were making for Spain in the 14 ton ocean-going vessel. It was when the *Memet* put in for fuel at St Paul de Leon on the Brittany coast that a fisherman from Guernsey recognised the stolen craft and called the police. The *Memet* was boarded by armed gendarmerie and the two men were detained. On board the boat two guns and ammunition were found. It was one of those guns which had killed John George.

During the period the two men spent in prison in Brest awaiting extradition to the UK, guards found a coded escape plot on Jason.

From it police learnt that the brothers planned to kidnap the British vice-consul when he came to visit them. They intended to use their hostage to bargain their way out of prison and onto an impounded Israeli gunboat which they meant to sail to Israel. Nothing, it seemed, could deter this arrogant pair.

In May 1980, Jason Richards and his elder brother Nicholas Manikum stood trial at the Central Criminal Court in a most intriguing case. The brothers themselves were and have remained a source of puzzlement to many. How was it that these two young men from a privileged home should commit so hideous and inexplicable a crime? Its lack of discernible motive still baffles those who consider the case.

There were, however, signs in their childhood that all was not well. Brought up in Wimborne in Dorset, they got themselves into endless trouble, until, in his teens, Nicholas had his first brush with the law and was sent to an approved school. His father, a recently retired bank official, and his mother ran an antique shop in Wimborne, but by the time Nicholas was released they had moved, along with Jason, to Minorca. Here they opened another antique shop.

Nicholas joined the family in Minorca and trained as a professional skin diver. Young as he was, but supremely confident of his own ability, Jason set up a substantial design and decorating business. Barely out of their teens, the brothers continued living with their parents in an antiques-filled villa in Sant Lluis, one of the whitest of white villages, a place of windmills, old farms and ancient customs. And what good days and nights they enjoyed, these two good-looking youngsters – fast cars, fast boats, fast life. They had all the trappings of real wealth. Perhaps it need never have ended.

But the local police began to receive complaints about the reckless and arrogant behaviour of the brothers. Smooth talkers, they appeared to think they could talk their way out of anything. There were car and motorcycle crashes, and Jason in particular seemed to demonstrate a yearning to live on the dangerous edge of things. His business began to fail. Debt began to pile up. On one occasion a garden centre owner, David Cox, was threatened by Jason and money was demanded of him. Cox was puzzled by the change in the boy's character. After the trial he had no hesitation in declaring, 'Jason had a psychopathic personality. Once he was a

The Richards brothers were arrested in France. Jason is on the right.

nice guy – happy and smiling. But during his last two years on the island he changed and seemed to get enjoyment only from taking terrible risks with his life.'

Minorca and its quiet charm and beauty was not enough for either of the brothers. The island with its beach parties and its ever so respectable expat community was far too bland for them. And anyway, Jason's business was £50,000 in debt and he was only 20 years of age. And Nicholas too, who had now adopted his mother's maiden name, was equally bored. There was more excitement for both of them beyond the tame shores of Minorca.

In the early months of 1979, the boys motored through France. At a hypermarket in Bayonne they bought two self-loading automatic rifles for £80 each. They sawed off the barrel of one of them so that it would fit snugly in a briefcase. Had they already decided that at some point they would carry out armed raids, that they might even do worse than that? On arriving in England, they drove round the south, eating, drinking and spending as some men in debt seem to be able to do.

On 21st April, now short of cash, they committed their armed robbery at the restaurant at Hoo St Mary, near Rochester. It was here that they played the Robin Hood characters, treating their victims with consideration, providing a cardigan, drinks, cigarettes and telling them not to worry as they would let the police know of their predicament.

And then only days later these were the men who arrived at Dunsfold and walked with John George into the copse where he met his death. Why did they kill him? Why did they go through the elaborate trussing up of this harmless man? The motive eluded the police at the time and presumably it does so today.

It is absolutely baffling.

Where did they pick up John George? Was it in Guildford, where he had a work-related appointment that morning? Did they threaten him with a gun as he was preparing to get into the Renault and did one of them – Jason most likely – sit in the car while George drove them to Dunsfold? But why did they pick on John George? He does not seem to have known them. Did the brothers pick up a total stranger knowing that they were going to kill him? And was it sheer chance that led them to a place that George knew through his work? Did he think that he might be able to get help there? Strangely, those who saw the three go into the wood had the impression that George was completely at ease and not at all concerned about his safety. He had a two-way radio in the Renault, which he might have used to call for help. But was he held at gunpoint? Or did he not know that he was in danger?

At the trial in May 1980 Mr Barry Hudson, QC for the prosecution, stated that 'Mr George was a lover of country things, particularly birds, but we cannot speculate why he went to that spot with two total strangers, and obviously went willingly. There is certainly nothing sinister in Mr George's conduct. At the time he met his death he was carrying on his lawful business.'

That is the central mystery of the Dunsfold murder.

In a dramatic turn-around during the trial, in which both men had denied any involvement, Nicholas changed his alibi and threw the blame on his younger brother. He claimed that Jason had told him that he and another man had committed the murder. Jason for his part advanced the alibi that the murder was committed at a time when he and Nicholas were having lunch together in Guildford.

Evidence was presented, however, that within hours of the murder Nicholas had called his former landlady, Mrs Jane Haberfield, in Bournemouth, and confessed. He said that Jason had shot George, although he seemed 'a very nice man'. He added, 'It was awful. I shall always remember his eyes.' But he never explained why it was that John George had met so dreadful a death.

After a withdrawal for four hours, the jury returned a verdict of guilty. Neither accused showed any emotion when sentenced to life terms. Perhaps they were comfortable with what they had done.

Mr Justice Mars-Jones, commenting on the failure to elicit any motive for this brutal crime, observed, 'Neither scientists nor medical men have developed any machinery to unlock the secret thoughts of a human being.'

After the trial Detective Chief Inspector Pat Crossan expressed the view that 'they were just a couple of pocket cowboys' who liked to think they were playboys, who were accustomed to a lavish lifestyle and who ran out of money. That may explain the restaurant robberies but it does not explain the murder of John George.

There are reasons to think that this killing was purely for kicks. Did the brothers do it solely for the buzz? But if so, did one of them first feel the need to commit this ghastly crime? Did one of them persuade the other how wonderful it would be to commit the ultimate crime, to wield the power of life and death, to demonstrate such superiority? If so, which brother exerted such influence over the other? And if so, was John George the nearest victim to hand?

Was this how it really was? Was it simply to experience what committing a murder felt like?

WHO KILLED SERGEANT GREEN?

17th June 1919 – Derby Day – Winner: Grand Parade.

A nd it's a great day, the first post-war Derby and back at Epsom, the race's rightful place, after four years' wartime exile at Newmarket. And the crowds are enormous as they always are. There are high rollers and cheap jacks; families and works outings; there's Pearly Kings and Pearly Queens. There are gipsies too, camping out for the week in their caravans and there's the usual run of three-card trick merchants, pitch-and-tossers, touts and tipsters. There's the most and the least respectable, some you could stake your life on and others, well . . . there's Billy Kimber's Brummagem mob and Darby Sabini's rival Clerkenwell gang, both of them 'protecting' the bookies, so they say. Then there are all the demobbed chaps back from Flanders and others still in uniform. There are Canadians in their bright blue hospital suits, white shirts, red ties. Not so far for them to come. They've just walked up to the course from the military convalescent camp at Woodcote Park just along the road. Wonderful day for everybody though, the Derby back at Epsom.

And at night, when the crowds have cleared, when the bookies, always last to go, are all packed up and gone, the place is quieter and the gipsy fires light up around the course. But down in the town the place still heaves with the crowds that have possessed it since Monday. And as with all crowds, there is good-natured banter and, as the night wears on, there are disagreements, not always serious of course, just enough to worry some bystanders, irritate others. Just enough at the Rifleman pub for instance at about 9.30 pm for someone to send for the police to pull two Canadians apart, to stop them brawling. Trouble is there are a couple of thousand up at Woodcote Park. You wouldn't think they were having hospital treatment, locals often think, not the way they behave, picking up our girls, drinking our beer and not behaving any better than our own lads. You'd think they'd behave better, wouldn't you, them being guests here?

In the ordinary course of events it would be the military police who came down to sort the men out. But in Epsom there are no military policemen. Not necessary, the powers-that-be must have thought. Not necessary for a convalescent camp. So it's the Epsom Borough police who get called in. And it's not easy because the two Canadians are reluctant to quieten down and they won't come quietly. They are eventually taken away but they make it difficult. And their comrades more or less accompany them, threatening the policemen, swearing at them, telling them that they won't get away with this. And when the two soldiers are taken inside and put in the cells, those outside make it clear they won't stand for it. They'll be back, they say. They're not going to put up with this.

The policemen are not without sympathy. To some extent they understand why the Canadian soldiers are so awkward, so difficult to deal with. The war has been over for months and they want to go home. They see the British soldiers being demobbed much more quickly than they. And hadn't the Tommies at least been able to come home on leave to see their families even during the fighting in France? But the Canadians have not seen their families since they left home. And they look at the American troops who have only been in Europe for a couple of years or so, and they are being shipped home as fast as can be. But not the Canadians. Not us, they grumble. Couldn't get us up to the front fast enough. Twenty thousand Canadian boys killed and God knows how many injured and maimed, but now it's all over there's no urgency to get us home. We've got to hang around here in a dull hutted camp with no indication when we shall ever see our families. Not that any of this was deliberate on the part of the authorities. The fact was that the naval transport needed to return home such large numbers of soldiers from all the dominions and colonies was severely stretched.

So yes, the policemen at Epsom did see the reason for the Canadians' grumbles. But at the same time they began to prepare themselves for further trouble. There'd already been trouble with servicemen in Folkestone at the beginning of the year and five had been killed in the Rhyl disorders. And there were 'khaki riots' over at Guildford, as well as in Plymouth, Dover, Bromley and Sutton. So it was best to be prepared. Inspector Charlie Pawley, in charge at Epsom, urgently called in officers from surrounding stations, making the number up to 16: himself, his veteran Station Sergeant Thomas Green, two other sergeants and a dozen constables. Some of these went on patrol around the town, clearing the streets, urging people to go home. Pawley also telephoned the camp and was told that everything was all right there but that there was a noisy mob along the road. Whether that was the twenty or so soldiers returning to Woodcote Park to send round the news of the arrest of their chums or whether it was the subsequently much larger mob on the way to effect a rescue is unclear.

It was a dry clear night. Had it been otherwise, there is little doubt that the urge to go down to Epsom would have fizzled out. But this was the best of summer weather. And men did not want to go to bed at 10.30. Odd really. Some of those up at Woodcote Park had fought hand to hand with the enemy under the stars. They had lain motionlessly in no man's land in the darkest hours. They had been out on midnight patrols. But at Woodcote Park, it was bed at 10.30. And this night the Canadians were little disposed to take notice of Last Post and Lights Out. Now they gathered in their tens and twenties, their fifties and hundreds. Tonight they listened to the most persuasive voices, the loudest voices, the angriest voices, encouraging them go down to the town to free their comrades.

The officer of the day, Major James Ross, did his best to calm the men. So did Regimental Sergeant Parsons. But they were ignored. Mobs listen to what they want to hear and they are not by their very nature inclined to hear those who counsel good sense. Mobs are deaf to reason. But up at Woodcote Park the Canadian mob heard the bugle sound 'Fall in' and the men fell in with a cheer. Up to four hundred of them set off down the road to Epsom. Not that all were bent on destruction and disorder. Doubtless many went along out of curiosity, or as 19 year old Private James Connors, one of the accused, was later to say for 'a jolly night'. But mobs breed their own follies and the men tumbled down the hill towards town, their shouts ever louder, their manner more threatening. Now they started heaving bricks at house windows and others armed themselves with stakes from the fences outside the Ladas Hotel, Ashley House and the Wesleyan Soldiers' Institute. For a mile and a half, all the way from the camp to the police station in Ashley Road, there was a trail of destruction. And all the while, right up to the gates of the police station, Major Ross and Regimental Sergeant Parsons endeavoured with little success to bring the men to order.

The number of police had been augmented by the time the mob reached the police station. Now there were 24 officers on duty, although they were still outnumbered by 16 to one. Major Ross urged the men to return to camp and Inspector Pawley joined him, explaining that the two prisoners would be charged with being drunk and disorderly but that this was more or less a minor matter. Surely, both Ross and Pawley tried to explain, it was not worth behaving in such a fashion. But such sound sense made no impression. There were more threats. The men should be released at once, reason or none. And then the police station would be burned down.

Then, there was a moment of hope. Major Ross would act as negotiator. He and Pawley decided to go inside the police station and work things out. But by now too many of those congregating outside wanted to create mayhem. The electric lights in the street and outside the station were stoned and then stones and sticks flew through the windows. Those officers who had stood their ground outside were forced into retreat.

Further attempts by Ross and Pawley were ineffective. They went outside again, the Inspector explaining that an ambulance was on its way to take the prisoners back to camp. And as the crowd surged forward Ross made his last unavailing plea.

All of the police were now inside the building. They heard the battering of the front door, heard the shattering of the windows, the angry cries of the men outside. Then, finding the front door too stubborn, some of the soldiers came down the narrow passageway at the side of the house. They worked at the iron bars of the windows, pulling them out of their sockets, and then climbed into the corridor inside. With a jemmy they freed one of the prisoners. Then the police officers regrouped and chased the invaders out of the building again.

It was now decided that with the rioters in retreat Inspector Pawley should lead a party of officers out of the back door to

The attack on the police station left a trail of broken windows and torn up railings.

charge the attackers from there. In fact this strategy did work and the rioters were further repulsed by nine policemen who charged them, flailing their truncheons. But the struggle went on. In the dark of the police station yard, fists, bricks, boots, stakes, truncheons were all employed. Pawley was struck on the head, Green fell to the ground, other officers were beaten and kicked, and the soldiers themselves took some heavy blows.

And at last, the mêlée petered out. The second prisoner was released from the cells and went to join his friends. Major Ross went over to Bugler Todd. 'For God's sake,' he said, 'blow something on your bugle.' And it worked. The men responded to the 'Fall in' for the second time that night. They fell in and marched back to camp. The Epsom riot was over.

Not quite over. Pawley was informed that some of the soldiers had carried Sergeant Green to a house opposite. He had been badly hurt. More than badly hurt. The doctor's report was to describe massive injuries to the skull. He was unconscious. An ambulance had been called. Sergeant Thomas Green, 51 years of age, his wife in hospital, father of two children, a police officer with 25 years' service behind him, never recovered consciousness. He had been booted in the head, some said. At least one other witness had seen him take a blow from either an iron bar or a stake which had felled him.

The following day Epsom viewed its wounds. The large double-fronted country residence which served as a police station looked, according to one witness, 'as though a Zeppelin had passed this way'. Every pane of glass in every window was shattered. The flagstones of the footpath had been ripped out and used to throw against the doors. The railings had been uprooted to serve as weapons. And to cap it all, from the attitude of the Canadians, there was likely to be a repeat. There were reports of them passing the police station and smiling and joking as if had been nothing more than 'a rag'. There were said to be threats of further trouble.

Now military police were drafted in to support the civil authority. Canadians were not allowed to pass the police station. All public houses were closed.

The investigation into the death of Station Sergeant Green was led by Divisional Detective Inspector John Ferrier with a team of five CID officers. There was some difficulty in identifying those who might be guilty as the lights had been out throughout the fracas and those who took part in it were not always sure about identification. But the military police, on the morning after the riot, identified seven or eight men who seriously merited further

Sgt Thomas Green (left) *and Inspector Charlie Pawley* (right).

questioning. They all bore signs of having been in a fight, all had head wounds. As Sir Richard Muir for the Crown was later to say in the Bow Street Magistrates court, 'The evidence of recent injuries to the head immediately after the riot is in my submission evidence that they took part in the riot. There they are like so many marked sixpences.'

Very many of the soldiers were questioned by the police and the statement of one of them, Private William Lloyd, went as follows: 'One of my chums, Eddie LePointe, who sleeps in hut No. 83, 4th Division, and next bed to me, told me that on Tuesday night on his getting to the camp gates about 11 pm, he saw a lot of Canadian soldiers dressed in blue, very excited, and Major Ross talking to them trying to quieten them, when a tall soldier said, "Let's go, boys!" and the crowd went and he (Eddie LePointe) went with them. He told me that on the way down they tore fences down; that he was in the middle of the crowd and saw the big soldier who had led them from the camp strike Sergeant Green with an iron bar over the side of his head, and the Sergeant fell down, and he heard somebody cry out, "Kick him," but he does not know whether that was done or not.'

So the police had an excellent witness. Even if Lloyd's account was, as hearsay, inadmissible in court, Eddie LePointe ought to bring real power to any prosecution case. And Lloyd had said something significant. It had not been publicly revealed that Green died from a blow from an iron bar. Until then, most believed that the policeman's skull had been shattered by a kick from an army boot. It was only later, after Lloyd's statement, that an iron bar was mentioned.

But Ferrier and his team did not pursue this matter until 21st June, four days after the killing. And by then, the Canadians had their stories ready. As for LePointe, he refused to admit to the account that Lloyd had alleged he had told him. Considering what Lloyd had said, LePointe's statement to the police is remarkable for its lack of precision. But there was no attempt made to bring Lloyd and LePointe together in order to analyse what each man had said.

But what about the murder weapon? It must have been discarded, probably near the police station or possibly somewhere along the route back to Woodcote Park. It was likely to be bloodstained, to carry fingerprints. But no iron bar was ever produced. The murder weapon ought to have been traceable. Was it ever seriously looked for?

And LePointe's story, as told by Lloyd, mentioned a tall soldier who had led the mob. He had called out, 'Let's go, boys!' and they had all followed him. And Eddie LePointe had gone with them. And it was this same tall soldier who had struck Sergeant Green with an iron bar on the side of his head.

So, call in the reluctant Eddie LePointe, who has so obviously clammed up. And let him see a line-up. Bring along ten or so other tall men and stick the tallest suspect from those arrested in the midst of them. Now, pick him out, Eddie.

But there was no line-up. The tallest man among the suspects, Allan McMaster, 6 feet tall, a former blacksmith, was never brought out for Eddie LePointe to identify.

After a hearing at Bow Street, seven Canadian privates were charged with rioting and the manslaughter of Sergeant Green. These were Frank Harold Wilkie 21; Alphonse Masse 27; Robert Alexander McAllan 45; James Connors 19; David Yerex 32; Robert Todd 20 and 27 year old McMaster.

At their trial at Guildford in July these seven men faced charges of riot and manslaughter. All claimed to have been in the vicinity of the riot but not as participants. Private Connors said that he had followed the crowd out of curiosity. In the ten minutes he was there he just heard a lot of shouting. Though Constable Rose had pointed out Connors as one of Green's assailants, this was not pursued in court.

Robert McAllan, a military policeman, said that when he saw what was going on at the police station and heard that it was going to be stormed, he said to someone, 'This is no place for me.' He set off back to camp and then he was hit on the head but he could not identify his assailant.

Allan McMaster and Alphonse Masse both said that they had followed the crowd but that they did not reach the police station. They admitted to seeing stones being thrown but they had not seen any policemen. Like McAllan both men suffered head injuries but they had no idea who had injured them.

Frank Wilkie like the others had just joined the crowd and when fifty or sixty men had gone into the station yard he tagged along. But he had not been involved in any fighting, he said. No, the wound on his head had certainly not been caused by a policeman's truncheon.

Todd said he that he sounded the bugle up at the camp because he was threatened. It wasn't to rally the men or anything like that. He had heard some men say that they were going to Epsom to free the prisoners. Then some of them had said they would ransack the town.

After a two-day trial all seven accused were acquitted of manslaughter. Five, however, were found guilty of riot. Bugler Todd and the military policeman, McAllan, were acquitted. The jury delivering its verdict asked the judge to bear in mind when sentencing that these men were not British subjects and that they might not understand our laws. Further they asked that His Honour be mindful of the men's military records.

Odd really, but perhaps the jury had been impressed by the raw innocence of these colonials. Innocent of the law? Was the jury under the impression that in Canada it was the custom to murder policemen by beating them violently with iron bars? As for their military service, only three of the guilty had been to France. Only one had been near the front line. And two were at Woodcote Park suffering not from war wounds but from venereal disease.

In the event Mr Justice Darling sentenced the five Canadians to twelve months' imprisonment without hard labour. After five months they were pardoned expressly by the Prince of Wales and sent home.

Does this not seem a trifle odd? Edward Shortland, a former Scotland Yard detective, who has thoroughly researched the case in recent years, is convinced that the truth of this grubby affair was hushed up at the highest levels of Government. It could not have occurred at a worse time, this murder, for that is what it was. It was in danger of fouling up plans for an official visit to Canada and the United States by the Prince of Wales. How would it seem if at the time the Prince was touring Canada one or more of its citizens was languishing in the death cell? Perhaps this explains the rather lacklustre investigation carried out by Divisional Detective Inspector John Ferrier. No urgency to question the suspects? No line-up? No murder weapon? And there was no call to the witness-box for Dr Thornely, who attended to Green as he lay in the hallway of the house opposite the police station and who later carried out the post-mortem? No one called from among the civilian population to say exactly what happened as the men marched on Epsom? Did someone lean on Ferrier? It is hard to resist that conclusion.

Edward Shortland's investigations, eighty years after the event, brought up another interesting fact. On Friday 26th June Private Frederick Bruns died up at the camp from a fractured skull. This was nine days after the death of the policeman. Had Bruns been involved in the fracas? And had he for several days kept his injuries to himself? Was he afraid to offer himself for medical treatment in case he was charged and put on trial? Whatever the case, the inquest on Bruns went through the Epsom Coroner's court on the Saturday, the day immediately after the soldier's death, but it was not linked in any way with that of Sergeant Green. The Coroner returned an open verdict and that was that.

Wouldn't it have caused a further embarrassment to the Prince if it had turned out that Bruns's death was the consequence of a blow from a British policeman's truncheon? And then, when it was recalled that Bruns was a citizen of the United States enlisted

The headstone over the grave of Sgt Thomas Green in Epsom cemetery.

in the Canadian army, would the reception of the Prince have been less than cordial in the United States?

It is not fanciful to imagine that the murder of Sergeant Thomas Green was smoothed over, covered up, in order not to ruin a royal progress which was intended as an acknowledgement of Canadian and American sacrifices in the war. It seems a most plausible sequence of events.

After all, didn't Allan McMaster, the tall former blacksmith, walk into the police station at Winnipeg ten years later? He had something on his mind, he said. He wanted to confess to murder. He had killed a policeman in England with a bar ripped from a cell window.

A telegram from Winnipeg to Scotland Yard read, 'Am detaining Allan McMaster, who admits being the murderer of Police Sergeant Green at Epsom on June the seventeenth nineteen nineteen. Do you want him? Wire instructions.'

The reply read, 'McMaster sentenced in connection with this affair and he is not wanted.'

No, that's all been cleared up. Don't open up that can of worms again.

17th June 1919 – Derby Day – Losers: Sergeant Green; then Epsom Borough Police Force and, lagging well behind the rest of the field, British Justice.

DEATH OF A NEWSAGENT

The high spot of Kevin Canty's day, 6th September 1976, was at about six o'clock in the morning. Whatever occurred after that, the interviews with the police, his name in the papers, all the celebrity with his school mates, could never match those scary early morning minutes. When the 15 year old arrived at 'Shelah's', he had been astounded to find the shop in darkness. He couldn't understand it. Mr Small was always there, always had the papers marked up in good time. But this morning the papers were still tied up in their bundles, in the shop doorway. Kevin peered in through the doorway, just in case Mr Small was there somewhere. Maybe he'd slept in. Maybe he'd turn on the lights any moment now and come through with some joke or other. Always had a joke with you, Mr Small.

But then a customer came along, one of the regulars. They agreed that Mr Small must have slept in and it wouldn't do him much of a favour to let him go on sleeping. They tried knocking on the door and shouting but there was no response. What about trying the fire alarm? That would get him out of bed quickly enough. But they couldn't get the alarm to work. What about phoning him? That seemed the next best idea. So they went over the road, young Kevin Canty and the customer, and called in at the supermarket. But there was no reply to their phone call and so now, rather concerned, they went back to 'Shelah's', this time accompanied by Ian Buchanan from the supermarket.

Together they went round the side to the back entrance. There was a light on inside. 'I peered in through a window at the back of the shop,' Buchanan said, 'and saw a trail of blood leading to the hall. I broke in through a small side window and saw Mr Small lying face down in the hall in a pool of blood. There was blood everywhere.'

The newsagent lay in the narrow hallway which led from the living quarters to the shop. He had been shot several times. There were three bullet wounds in his chest and one in his head.

But who on earth would want to shoot Geoffrey Small in his quite modest little newsagent's shop in Westmead Road? A murder in Sutton? It's really not that kind of place. This part of Sutton regarded itself as a village. Forget that it is part of London. Sutton has more homely roots and, if Sutton was a village, then Geoffrey Small was its village newsagent. And he was such a decent chap. Everyone seemed to like him. And everyone round here knew him well because before Geoffrey took over the business five years earlier, his father had owned 'Shelah's'. He was reliable and hardworking, so much so that he and his wife Joyce had been able to open another shop, The Drug Store, on the other side of the road. They were thriving and deservedly so. And people who work hard, people who prosper in their businesses, even if there is the slightest scintilla of envy, are not normally done to death in this way. It was unaccountable. The police were equally baffled as to who might have carried out what they acknowledged to be a highly efficient killing.

The police team, led by Detective Superintendent Bevan Moss, considered how the killer had gone about his task. He had walked down the side passage to the back of the house. Here on the ground floor was a diamond-leaded window which looked out onto the back garden. Evidently the intruder had chosen not to smash the glass but instead had eased up the lead flashing and had taken out a small lozenge of glass next to the window catch. He had then been able to open the window. He had left no fingerprints either round the window or later elsewhere in the house. Outside there was a small footprint, too indistinct to reveal anything other than that it was a plimsole. On the seat of an armchair just inside the window, was an equally indistinct but similar foot pattern.

And the bloody footprints on the floor? These were Small's, as the dying man, acting on reflex as much as anything after taking three shots to his chest, had tried to stagger to the telephone.

It was here, in the dark room at the rear of the house, that Geoffrey Small's murderer had waited for him. And it was obvious to the police that he knew his victim's habits. He knew that Small would arrive at about 5.30 am. He knew that he would enter the shop, not by the front door but by the rear, because the shop was burglar-alarmed. Anyone coming into the shop by the front entrance would have to cross the shop floor and then go through the communicating door to the living quarters at the back, where the switch to the alarm was located. But this took too long. By now the alarm would have triggered. Geoffrey Small always entered his shop by the door at the rear, which gave him time to switch off the alarm before it was activated.

This morning, as every morning in the three months since he had moved to nearby Cheam, Geoffrey Small parked his red Volvo outside the shop, came down the side passageway and let himself in by the rear door. And it was then that his waiting killer shot him. He fired six bullets, three of which lodged in the unsuspecting man's body. When Small had staggered into the hallway he had slumped to the ground and it was then that his executioner had fired another bullet into the back of his head.

And the killer? He took with him a plastic bag containing the weekend's takings of about £150 and a few cheques. Perhaps he also took Small's wallet, which was not known to contain very much, although Fenton Bresler, the *Sunday Express* legal correspondent, was to hazard the guess that it did contain something significant which the murderer or his employer wanted. But that seems far-fetched.

What then was it all about? Was this obviously highly planned offence, carried out in such ruthless style, simply to relieve a shopkeeper of such a paltry sum? Was it all for £150? Or was the theft of the money to throw police off the scent, to conceal the real reason for the killing? That is part of the mystery of the murder of Geoffrey Small.

And now, this murderer, does he race off like some drug-crazy kid, panicking as he hurries out? Not at all. This man is organised. He is methodical. He has committed a most awful deed, an act of the greatest callousness. But he is not thrown by this. He leaves by the rear door, closing it after him. He walks down the side passage and lets himself out of the gate which he closes behind him. And there in front of him, just outside the shop is a customer, one of the early morning regulars, waiting for Geoffrey Small to open up.

'Good morning,' says the customer, for that is how people greet each other in the silence of the early morning streets before the day reminds us to ignore each other.

Geoffrey Small
(*Sunday Express*)

'Good morning,' says the murderer quite agreeably, turning left up Westmead Road.

The customer thought no more of it at the time, save that he was one of the few in the know. The Smalls had moved to Cheam. They were no longer living in the flat and they had told only very few people. Perhaps, thought the customer, they had let the flat; perhaps this was their new tenant. But he only caught a fleeting glimpse of the man. When the police later asked him what he recalled, he was able to give them a few indicators but not enough for a photofit. He thought the man was about 5 feet 6 inches tall and of slim build. His brown hair was brushed across the top of his head and rather frizzy at the front. He wore a check sports jacket and brown trousers. The customer thought that the man he had seen and spoken to was about 45 years of age. Not much to go on there really. It would fit very many of the forty-odd-year-old, male population. But it was not some gun-happy kid out to rob a newsagent, the police knew now. There was something different about this whole business.

At about the time of the murder, a woman living in Sutton Grove, just round the corner from the shop, heard a man running down the road. He got into a parked car and drove off at high speed. The killer? Probably. At that time of morning there were no crowds to mingle with, no streams of commuters or shoppers to get lost in. He needed to make a fast getaway and therefore it does seem likely that he had parked his car near to the newsagent's shop.

What very quickly struck Superintendent Bevan Moss's team of investigating officers was how different this killing was from the majority of shootings. It was the scale of the planning, the awareness of the victim's movements, the knowledge that Small had moved house, the murderer's carefully planned entry and his cool exit that alerted the detectives to the fact that this killer might be a professional assassin. And when they inspected the bullets, when they worked out the pattern of the firing of the gun, they knew that this was no common-or-garden murderer. This was cold and calculated. This was no-run-of-the-mill robbery even though the weekend's takings had been taken.

But who would want to kill such a man in so calculated a manner? It all seemed so out of keeping with the kind of man that Geoffrey Small undoubtedly was. 'My husband was extremely ambitious but he was very popular in the district,' Joyce Small told a local reporter. 'He was a real comedian. He used to make all the kids who came in laugh. His motto was: When you go through the shop door, it's like going on stage.'

Some days after the killing Detective Superintendent Moss told a reporter that this murder was unique in Sutton. It was more like Soho than Sutton, he said. 'We have never had a killing like this,' he continued. 'We are baffled by the motives behind this brutal killing, which had an air of professionalism about it.'

When the bullets were dug out of the wall they were found to be small, nickel 9mm (7.65 calibre) bullets. They were foreign, Austrian probably, expensive and normally used by specialists.

The gun, a semi-automatic pistol which was never found, was not the type used for target shooting. It was a deadly stopping weapon, the kind of side arm used by bodyguards, a Browning or a Walther .320. This was no 'Saturday night special', picked up in a pub for a few pounds. It was not some old wartime frightener. Whoever used this kind of gun employed it for the purpose of killing. And it could only be fired effectively by a trained professional. In the hands of an amateur it would be wildly inaccurate, for the cartridge ejection mechanism operated with such force that it jerked the gun arm.

After his retirement, Bevan Moss explained to Fenton Bresler that he was in no doubt that a trained gunman had killed Geoffrey Small. 'Anybody but an absolute professional would find it very difficult hitting the target,' the detective said. 'This bloke adopted what we call the double tap method of firing, in as much as he fired two shots, bang-bang, and then changed position, bang-bang again. We could tell that from the marks on the wall where the cartridges had hit.'

His work completed, the murderer, that skilled practitioner, had calmly collected five of his expended cartridges but failed to pick up two others which had lodged behind an extractor grille on the wall.

Who were the police looking for then? The SAS are trained to use the double tap method because of its effectiveness. At one point the murder was described as 'an IRA-style murder'. Was there some connection with Ireland? One lead certainly suggested that there was. Only hours after the shooting, a man had called at a house not far from where Small had recently lived. The man claimed to know Small and said he wished to trace him. But the people who answered the door to the enquirer had not heard of the newsagent and said they could not help. Only later did they realise that they had been asked about the dead newsagent.

The description, the police thought, seemed to fit a former friend of the Small family who had in 1971 retired after 21 years in the local police force. Apparently an IRA supporter, he had gone to live in Ireland and was traced and interviewed by the Garda. He was asked about his movements on 6th September but the enquiry led nowhere.

Several other potential suspects were interviewed – men known to the police for using firearms. A man who had left Sutton on the day of the murder was traced to Glasgow but he was cleared of any involvement. Certain mercenaries were known to be assassins for hire, their going rate for the job being estimated at that time up to £2,000. In November 1976, after police through Europe and the Middle East had been urged to assist in the search, a former mercenary, a 28 year old man who had formerly served in the SAS, was held. But this trail led nowhere. The man was picked up, questioned and released.

Had there been a mistake somewhere? Had the assassin killed the wrong man? Had he really been seeking to eliminate Bertie Smalls, a supergrass under police protection, whose information, to save his own skin, had led to the imprisoning of several bank robbers? There was certainly an underworld contract out on Bertie Smalls. But this was too absurd a theory. No one could possibly imagine that Geoffrey Small, Sutton newsagent, was Bertie Smalls, a notorious full-time criminal. Nor would a highly organised hunter like the man who committed the murder in Sutton make such an elementary error.

The police were undoubtedly baffled. There was nothing in Small's background to indicate why he should be the target of a professional hitman. There was no one that anyone knew of who would wish to get rid of so popular a man.

And yet, one fact nags away. It's odd. Just a little thing really. Or is it?

In June 1976 the Smalls had moved from the flat to a house in Cheam. Nothing remarkable in that. But why was it kept such a secret? Why did the Smalls tell so few people about their move? The paper boy Kevin Canty thought his boss had slept in and he and the regular customer who had tried with Kevin to set off the alarm had been under the impression that the Smalls still occupied the house. Was the reason for such secrecy that they feared burglary if it became known that the house was empty? Or was there some deeper seated reason?

At the inquest, held over a year later, one of the part-time assist-ants in the shop said that for the past six months Mr Small had seemed worried about something. But she could not say what.

Was there some problem over a woman? Was Geoffrey Small a ladies' man who had offended some husband or boyfriend? There was certainly some local gossip but a relationship that he had had with a woman was now over. And Joyce Small was frank with the reporter from the *Sutton Herald*. 'My husband was a ladies' man,' she admitted. 'He loved women, talking and joking with them. But I would like people to know that whatever went on, he and I were very happy together. We both worked hard and kept our marriage together for the sake of the children. Did he have other relationships? I do not know. I do not want to know. There is no point.'

And when the police followed up this aspect of his life they came to another dead end.

The *Sutton Herald*'s offer of £1,000 for information produced no results. But the offer still apparently stands. And the murder of Geoffrey Small is as great a mystery now as it was when at six o'clock one morning over quarter of a century ago Kevin Canty first peered in the front door of the darkened shop.

THE PIRBRIGHT TRAGEDY

It's one of those villages that you wish you lived in as you drive through. You see the green, the duck pond, the old church, the two venerable pubs, the elegant houses, many of them listed, the vast common and you tell yourself that this is a place where you could be happy, where you could settle down, enjoy life. Could anything ever go wrong in such a place? Well, yes. Something went dreadfully wrong in Pirbright on Tuesday 11th February 1958.

The Storeys lived in one of those handsome houses, a 400 year old converted, red-brick farmhouse overlooking the green. Like so many of his neighbours, George was a highly successful businessman, a partner in a firm of City accountants, but a quiet enough chap for all that, happy at weekends pottering round his extensive garden. And his wife, Helena, did 'good works', helping the aged and the sick, organising a village savings group. And there was a boy, Alec, now 19 years old, tall and fair-haired, 'a quiet, pleasant youngster', according to one local. 'We've often seen him about on his motorbike.'

In that second week of February, Alec was coming to the end of his 14 days' leave. He was doing his two years' National Service with the East Surrey Regiment and had been stationed in Germany but when his leave ended he was to report to his unit in Bury St Edmunds.

On Saturday night, the Storeys had held a rock-and-roll party for Alec in their garage, and the next day the young soldier and his mother had taken the empties back to the public house across the green. And on the Monday she was at the greengrocers', buying fruit for Alec's return journey to Bury St Edmunds. It was all so predictably normal.

During the morning of 11th February, a Tuesday, Helena and her son were seen walking arm in arm across the green. He was due to report to Bury St Edmunds later in the day.

At 2.20 pm, Alec turned up at Knaphill police station on his motorcycle. He went inside and seemed at first not to know what to say. The policeman on duty reported that the young man just stood there in silence and then he had undone his raincoat and had taken a .22 automatic pistol from the waist band of his trousers.

'I've just shot my mother,' he said. 'She is lying dead in the bedroom.'

He handed the pistol to the policeman. 'Careful,' he said. 'It's loaded.'

He fumbled in his pockets for a key. It fitted the back door, he told the policeman.

'I put a lot of bullets in her head,' he said.

When the police went to the house they found Mrs Storey in her son's bedroom. There were five bullet wounds in her skull. Later that day, and without any hesitation, Alec made a statement which amounted to a confession.

He told how he had borrowed the gun that morning from a neighbour. He had wanted some target practice. He had asked his mother about borrowing the gun and she was quite agreeable to the idea. After all, he was a soldier, wasn't he? He was grown up. He could look after himself.

Sometime after lunch, at about two o'clock, Alec said, he had been up in his bedroom. He was playing with the gun, twiddling it round his middle finger when suddenly it went off. He had failed to engage the safety catch. The bullet went right through the floor. He ran downstairs to the dining room and found the floor coated with a mass of ceiling plaster. Then his mother came in, horrified at the mess and doubtless alarmed by the report of the gun. They went upstairs to look at the damage in his bedroom. It has not been revealed precisely what Helena Storey said but one may assume that her response would be no different from that of most other mothers who had found similar havoc in the house.

Did she rant about carelessness? It would be remarkable if she did not. Did she perhaps say something about it being time he acted more responsibly? Surely she did. Did she use words such as ' . . . not fit to . . .', ' . . . absolutely tired of it . . .', '. . .glad when you get back to barracks . . .', '. . .worse than useless. . .'? If she did so, then she used words little different from those uttered by many an angry mother in such a situation.

'My mother was very upset about the damage,' the statement continued. 'She said she had a good mind to pack up and leave the house as Mr Storey would be very annoyed and she did not want any more rows. She was on her knees looking at the bullet hole. While she was like this I pulled the trigger which resulted in her being hit in the head. She jerked forward straightaway and fell over on her tummy. I aimed a second shot at her head. And then I emptied the magazine at her head in panic, with the exception of one round. I think the first shot killed her because there was no sign of her breathing. I emptied the magazine because I thought if she was not dead she might be crippled for life. After I had done it I felt light-headed but quite normal.'

Later in his statement Alec mentioned that he believed that his mother was going blind. That was a terrible fate, he believed. And he seemed to think that his solution to the problem was appropriate. 'I thought it would be best to kill her for her own sake,' he explained.

Alec Taylor Lawrence was charged with the murder of Helena Storey. It was an enormous shock for Pirbright. It seemed inconceivable. As more than one local said, 'The family have always seemed very happy.'

And the charge brought another surprise. Most people had assumed that Alec was the natural son of the Storeys but it now transpired that he was a foster child. More of his early history was revealed at the Magistrates Court hearing at Woking and later at his trial at the Old Bailey. How Alec Lawrence came to be with the Storeys needed to be told in both courts as it served to explain so much about the tragic affair.

In 1941, Alec, then aged two, was living in North London with his natural parents, the Lawrences. One night during the Blitz the district was heavily bombed and the Lawrences' house collapsed. Fortunately, both parents and Alec were dug out of the wreckage.

The Storeys, already a comfortably-off couple, with a strong social conscience, lived nearby and, hearing of the plight of the now homeless Lawrences, offered to look after Alec, who was the youngest of several children. The child's parents, whose background and financial position were significantly different from the Storeys, were not heartless people. They cared for all of their children but they were undeniably poor and were grateful to the Storeys for their offer. They could give the baby so much. He would have a wonderful chance in life, they could see that. Nevertheless, although Alec went to live with the Storeys with his parents' blessing, they would not permit his adoption but the agreement, though, seems to have been admirably managed.

From now on Alec lived in an entirely different kind of home, at first in North London and later in Pirbright. His foster parents were determined that he should be well educated and sent him to Mill Hill, a public school of some standing. At home he mixed with other children and young people equally privileged.

All the time, the Storeys were aware of their position, alive to the fact that Alec was someone else's child. In consequence they encouraged him to pay occasional visits to his real family and, when the Lawrences moved to the north of England, to spend holidays with them. How sensible of them. But for Alec, maintaining links with his own parents and his brothers and sisters was to become, as he grew older and increasingly away

Alec Lawrence (Daily Mail)

from them, a wholly uncomfortable experience. What can it have been like for him, passing from one kind of world to another? Such a contrast, such demands on him to be at ease in two very different households. How did the public schoolboy with the well-honed vowels feel in the company of his kin? Did he shudder at their dropped aitches? Did he squirm at what he perceived to be the crudeness of their accents, the poverty of their vocabulary, the limits of their aspirations? Was this the root of the trouble with at least one of his brothers? For how did the siblings regard him? As an alien? Did they welcome him or did his plummy tones arouse their scorn and anger? Did the way they held their knives and forks shame him? Did his manner strike them as toffee-nosed? Was this where Alec really belonged, he must constantly have asked himself, with these people with whom he had so little empathy?

Unsurprisingly, at Alec's trial in May 1958, great play was made of the emotional distress he had suffered as a consequence of his position, a boy who felt himself a member of neither world. He felt the disloyalty towards his own mother and father, wished that he could love and admire them as he loved and admired the Storeys. And whose fault was all of this? Didn't the blame attach to some degree to Mrs Storey who had placed him in this position? These people whom he so loved, they weren't parents, he had told himself. They were simply benefactors.

Was this the reason why some months earlier he had attempted suicide? This was briefly referred to at the trial, described by Detective Sergeant Henry Helsdon as 'some sort of attempt to commit suicide with a gun'. It may be that Helena Storey had never known about it. Possibly it was not known to anyone until Alec confessed to the police. If Mrs Storey had been aware that Alec had tried to kill himself, it is unlikely that she would have given her permission for him to borrow the pistol from her neighbour. But an attempt at suicide, if it was made, does point to a deeply unhappy young man.

Other references were made at the trial to Alec's relatively modest examination results. Three years earlier he had sat for his GCE and had failed in three subjects. He had felt that despite all their efforts on his behalf he had let down the Storeys. 'I was convinced,' Alec's statement read, 'I had been a great disappointment to her.' In consequence, he had lost weight and a physician had diagnosed an anxiety state.

Mr F. H. Lawton QC, defending Alec at the Old Bailey, posed fundamental questions about the source of the accused lad's unhappiness. 'We are all familiar with the story of Cinderella and the ugly sisters and how the fairy godmother came along with results no doubt delectable to Cinderella,' Lawton said. That was Part One of the story. But then he asked, 'What would have happened to Cinderella if the fairy godmother had not come on the scene?' That was more likely in his view of the world. 'In real life, away from the fantasies of childhood, fairy godmothers do not turn up.'

But here, in the Alec Lawrence story, the fairy godmother might be said to have turned up. All the same, everything did not end happily ever after. Part Two of the story had brought emotional distress for a boy who felt that he did not really belong to anyone and who was convinced that he had disappointed his benefactors and was a failure. Alec Lawrence, his counsel opined, was a disappointed Cinderella, suffering from a mental abnormality which substantially impaired his ability to appreciate fully the nature of his actions.

The *Daily Mirror* very much liked the Cinderella analogy. On 9th May, reporting the outcome of the trial, its headline read: 'The Cinderella Mind of a Boy Killer'.

But what about the other reason for killing his foster mother that Alec had cited in his statement, his concern that she was going blind? Much was made of this as evidence of Alec's irrationality. Mr Lawton said that Mrs Storey had been recommended to wear stronger spectacles and that Alec had become obsessed with the erroneous idea that she was going to lose her sight completely. There was apparently a rumour in the village that Mrs Storey was going blind and presumably this had emanated from Alec. Mr Lawton asked Dr Walter Neustatter, a Harley Street psychiatrist, called by the defence, if the young man's obsession with his foster mother's loss of sight indicated an abnormality of mind which substantially prevented his reasoning process.

Dr Neustatter told the court that when he interviewed the prisoner in Brixton prison, Alec had told him blindness was the worst possible thing that could overtake anybody, and if his mother – so he called her – became blind she would not have been able to see any of the things that made life worthwhile. He was doing her a kindness, Alec said, relieving her of suffering. According to Dr Neustatter, Alec was incapable of marshalling any of the obvious arguments against killing her.

Another Harley Street consultant, Dr Clifford Allen, who interviewed Alec in Brixton on three occasions, gave it as his opinion that the young man was suffering from the very early stages of schizophrenia.

Dr Alastair McCall said he had known Alec from childhood. He was a shy boy, one who tended not to join in easily with other children. And then, in adolescence, the doctor said, 'He became rather noisy, rather excessively colourful in dress, had long hair and obviously took a delight in exhibitionism.'

Perhaps such changes would manifest less surprise these days, nearly fifty years on. Yet did they signify some inner disturbance? Or is it more likely that the boy simply felt the need to assert himself or more likely still that he was undergoing a common adolescent transformation?

Even Mr L.G. Scarman QC, for the prosecution, acknowledged the problems that beset the young man in the dock. He saw fully that there was a tension, that Alec Lawrence was torn, pulled in two directions by his competing loyalties to his parents and his guardians.

After two days the jury retired and returned a verdict of guilty of manslaughter on the grounds of diminished responsibility. He was sentenced to three years' imprisonment.

Addressing Alec before passing sentence, Mr Justice Ashworth said, 'The jury have taken a view which was abundantly justified ... Nonetheless, I have to deal with you for the crime and the possibility of its repetition.' It was the minimum sentence, and justly so.

There is little doubt that there was abundant and deserved sympathy for Alec Lawrence, a young man for whom the tugs of love and guilt proved to be too much. Some killings arouse the utmost revulsion. In this case, however, one cannot but feel for both victim and killer.

THE TOWPATH MURDERS

It was a dullish sort of day. Not at all like summer. But perhaps as he cycled along the towpath that Monday, 1st June 1953, George Coster had his mind on other matters. Perhaps the maintenance inspector was thinking less about the condition of the lock walls and more about the next day's marvellous event. For the young queen was to be crowned and, so they were saying, this was to herald a new Elizabethan age. Anyway it was to be such a wonderful occasion, a symbolic step away from the seemingly endless grim austerity that had followed the awful tragedies of the war. It was a time of such hope for the future. And perhaps the Costers were going to watch the coronation of Elizabeth II on television. Just think, on television . . .

But whatever he was thinking about no doubt changed at about quarter past eight, for that was when he saw the body in the water. He was more or less opposite Twickenham, on the Richmond side of Teddington Lock. He at once called the police and a river patrol boat came to carry the body ashore.

It was a girl. There were knife wounds to her chest and back, a stab wound in the face, and her skull was fractured. And she had been raped. But who was she? No one had been reported missing.

A search along the towpath revealed a spot near Teddington Lock – a thicket known as Lovers' Glade – where the grass was trampled down and bloodstained. Marks in the gravel suggested that the murder had taken place there and that the body had been dragged 20 yards to the slope of the river bank and thrown in the water. It was estimated from the flow of the water and the location of the body, half a mile away from the murder site, that this had occurred about midnight.

Then the searchers found shoes. Two pairs. Of different sizes.

Was there a second body? Had two girls been slain here? There was no sign of a second body.

Under the direction of Detective Chief Inspector Hannam, house-to-house enquiries began on both sides of the river. Could anyone identify a girl who had worn a yellow tartan blouse, blue serge slacks, white socks and black shoes?

Police launches began dragging the river while the grass along the river bank was scythed in the search for the murder weapon. Or were they, the police already began to wonder, faced with a murderer who had not thrown away his knife? Was there the prospect of a killer who would attack again? And again? For this was no ordinary murderer. Chief Superintendent Bill Rudkin told the crime reporter Duncan Webb, 'In my 28 years on the job I've watched post-mortems on a few murdered bodies. But this is the work of a maniac. This murderer is a monster.' And it seemed that he was a monster of the most terrifying strength. From his inspection of the stab wounds Dr Arthur Mant, the pathologist, confirmed that the police were looking for a man of unusual strength.

At seven that night, Mrs Gertrude Songhurst of Princes Road, Teddington, who had reported her 16 year old daughter Barbara missing, identified the body. She had seen Barbara with her friend Christine Reed on the Sunday afternoon and thought the girls had spent the night together at Christine's house at Roy Grove, Hampton Hill. She was such a good girl, her mother was to say, always so cheerful. And she had been looking forward to Coronation night so much because she had entered a bathing beauty contest organised by Teddington and Hampton Wick Coronation Celebration Committee.

And now it was revealed that Christine too had not returned home that night. Her parents had imagined that their 18 year old daughter was sleeping at Barbara Songhurst's house. But neither home had a telephone, so that the parents had simply assumed that their daughters were safe. The factory where Christine worked reported that she had not appeared on the Monday, just as Barbara had not turned up at the chemist's shop where she worked.

And where were the girls' cycles? Where was Christine's blue and cream BSA racing model? What had happened to Barbara's maroon and silver cycle with the semi-drop handlebars? There was no sign of them. And then, the next day, on 2nd June, as the Queen's coach went in procession to Westminster Abbey, police dragging the Thames found Christine Reed's cycle. It lay on the river bed, about 100 yards upstream from where the attack took place.

But the search for Christine went on, while Chief Inspector Hannam built up a picture of the girls. The detective established that both were 'virtuous, clean-living girls, both fond of dancing and the company of boys'. On Saturday night they had been to a dance but they had not on the Sunday gone out to meet anyone they had met dancing. The girls, the police found out, had passed much of the Sunday with three Twickenham boys, the youngest aged 18, the oldest 21, who were camping on the Surrey side of the river. As usual on summer weekends there were very many young campers on the land between Teddington Lock and Petersham.

The girls had called on the three boys in the morning and in the afternoon, and sometime about 8 o'clock they had gone to the tents again. They had had such a good day. They had talked; they had sung songs, told jokes, played tricks on each other. There was general horseplay, chasing, hiding, some kissing of a not very serious nature. And then, the girls had decided that it was time to go home. The time? Lateish. It was very dark. The boys could not be certain. None of them had a watch. 11 o'clock possibly. Maybe a bit earlier. Maybe a bit later. As vague as that. But the murder site was no more than three quarters of a mile from the boys' camp, only minutes away by cycle.

Several witnesses on the towpath at that time were equally uncertain. One had heard a scream but he could not be precise. But then one man who was a reliable witness turned up. He had seen two girls on cycles at 11.30. So now the police felt confident that death had occurred between that time and midnight.

So where was Christine and where was Barbara's cycle? Where too was the murder weapon? Hundreds of statements were taken over the next three weeks. Questionnaires were left first of all at 500 houses on the Ham Estate but later these were extended much more widely, to people living within a radius of several miles of the murder scene. Convinced that they were looking for a local man, Hannam hoped for useful information. But the questionnaires produced very little of value save the time when the

Herbert Hannam, the Detective Chief Inspector in charge of the case.

murder had taken place received further confirmation. In the course of two weeks police took 1,650 statements but none provided the essential clue. In their search for the elusive murder weapon, electro-magnets were used to drag the river but it was to no avail.

At one o'clock on the afternoon of Saturday 6th June, Christine Reed's body was found floating in mid-stream near Glover's Island, a considerable distance from Teddington Lock but close to Richmond. Just like Barbara, she had been attacked with the utmost savagery, though it was evident from the cuts on her arms that she had put up a fierce struggle. She had been stabbed several times in the chest and back and her skull was fractured. She too had been raped. All the evidence suggested that when she was thrown in the water, she was still alive.

The knife wounds in Christine's body were identical to those in Barbara's. One weapon. One murderer. That much was now certain. The search for the weapon continued, and on 10th June a three-mile stretch of the river was drained but nothing of value was found and after nearly a fortnight the police were no nearer to identifying the killer than they had been in the first hours.

The police now had, however, a clearer picture of what had occurred on the towpath. The girls must have been cycling one in front of the other. They had come to a large tree where the path divided. One girl had continued on the main towpath while her friend had taken the other path round the tree.

It was at that point that the first girl had been knocked off her cycle with a fierce blow. And then the second, unsure of what had happened to her friend, dismounted. And then she was felled. Had the murderer, Hannam wondered, thrown some kind of weapon at the second girl while at the same time attacking the first?

Hannam was sure that the man was local. It was not someone who had travelled after the deed by public transport, for he would be too dishevelled and conspicuous for that. In fact he could not have had far to go at all, for he ran the risk of being spotted in the street, his hands red, his shirt, his trousers deeply stained with blood. Had he taken Barbara's cycle? And he was someone who knew the location well, who knew where to hide, where to attack, where to be rid of two victims.

There was, Hannam and his colleagues began to think, some similarity between the double murder and the violent rape of a schoolgirl on Oxshott Heath on 24th May. A man with a cycle had hit her on the back of the head with an axe and dragged her into bushes. The girl had told her attacker that she was only 14 but he had ignored that. She remembered that the man had a cleft chin.

And then, on 11th June, a 49 year old woman, walking her dog in Windsor Great Park, was asked for directions to a local pub by a young man on a cycle. When she turned away from him to point the way, he had put his hand over her mouth and forced her into the bushes. Quick-witted, she told him that she had recently had a major operation and he relented. Instead, he asked her for 'a little kiss', and had then taken 17 shillings out of her purse. He had warned her not to shout for help because he had a knife and knew how to throw it. He then cycled away.

This had a similarity to the Oxshott Heath attack and Hannam thought it worth comparing the two attacks. Both victims described their attacker as short but strongly built. He had a deep cleft in his chin and wavy hair. He had ridden a bike and had attacked both of his victims from behind. The schoolgirl said that he had carried a meat cleaver; the housewife said that he had had a knife.

Was this the man who had murdered the girls on the towpath? He had said to the woman in Windsor Great Park that he knew how to throw a knife. Had he thrown a knife at one of the girls on the towpath while he attended to the other? Or had he thrown a meat cleaver?

Roy Tarp, a schoolteacher from Greenford, read about this police theory and reported that some weeks earlier he had met a man on the towpath who was throwing knives and an axe, using the trees for target practice. He had seemed a real expert. Tarp was so impressed that he asked if he might throw the knives and the man had allowed him to do so. But the schoolteacher had not been successful. He had missed the target completely with the knife he had been given – a Gurkha kukri – and it had been lost in the waters of a gravel pit. The man had waded into the pit but failed to find his knife.

Anything else? Tarp was asked.

Well, the man had been wearing nothing but white shorts and gym shoes. Perhaps that was understandable as it was summer. But then he had climbed the trees and had swung so easily from branch to branch. It took such strength and skill. Just like Tarzan really.

When Hannam followed up this information, he must have hoped that he would find a vital clue in the gravel pit but that was not to be.

On 17th June, two policemen in a patrol car, alerted by two workmen who believed they had seen someone answering the description of the murderer, picked up a man on Oxshott Heath. At Kingston police station he identified himself as Alfred Charles Whiteway, aged 22, a labourer at present unemployed. He was married and had a year old daughter. Because housing was so expensive, he and his wife lived apart, he with his parents at Sydney Road in Teddington, she with her parents in Kings Road, Kingston. But they did see each other every day.

Asked what he was doing at Oxshott, Whiteway gave the police the name and address of a friend he was going to see. This story checked out satisfactorily and he was allowed to go home. Four days later, reading the the report of Whiteway's apprehension, Hannam decided to call him in for further questioning.

This time Whiteway was put in a line-up. The housewife and school girl both identified him as the man who had attacked them. Roy Tarp, the schoolteacher, recognised him as the man whom he had met throwing knives on the towpath.

'So help me, sir,' Whiteway said when asked about the murders, 'I don't know a bloody thing about them. The bloke that did them was mad.'

Alfred Whiteway

But Hannam was confident that he now had the towpath murderer in custody and charged him with the rape on Oxshott Heath and the assault in Windsor Great Park. His enquiries encouraged him to think he had the right man. Whiteway had been in Approved School, admittedly not for violence but for theft. The report of the Head described him as 'foul mouthed, cruel to animals and lethargic'.

Hannam recalled the cleft chin and noted that Whiteway lived near the towpath, only seven minutes ride on his flashy blue cycle; so many things about the man seemed to point to him as the monster the detective sought.

For here was a man obsessed with knives, a man who often tucked a sheath knife into the top of his boot and who regularly carried others in the saddle bag of his bicycle. When he worked on the railway Whiteway had used railway sleepers as targets. As a packer at Decca Records at New Malden, he was remembered for throwing knives at packing cases. Knife throwing had been a hobby since childhood and Whiteway could split a matchbox at 30 yards. One girl who knew him said that it was all he could think of. 'It was knives, knives, knives.'

With an axe Whiteway could hit a chalk line on a tree from 40 yards. And there were more stories of him playing Tarzan in the trees along the towpath, of climbing up the scaffolding on building sites using only his hands. Former workmates said that he often spent his lunch hours weight lifting. But not every lunch hour. He had been working on a building site at Woodmansterne in March 1952, when, one lunchtime at nearby Oxshott Heath, a woman with her child in a pram was hit on the head with a lead pipe. Police had questioned him about this.

Whiteway now admitted the rape of the schoolgirl. 'I did assault her,' he said. 'I don't know what made me do it.' And he had also attacked the housewife.

But for the night of the murder of the two girls Whiteway had an alibi. His wife, pregnant with their second child, told police that they had been in Canbury Gardens until about 11.30 and then her husband had walked her home. They had had a cup of tea at the back door – Whiteway was barred from the house by his mother-in-law – and then he had returned to Teddington via Kingston Bridge. He had not cycled along the towpath because it was dark and he had therefore preferred to take the longer route home. Hannam doubted the truth of this alibi and it was later demolished.

But Hannam had failed to locate either the knife or the axe. It was imperative that he find them. Whiteway's sister, however, confirmed that a black-headed meat cleaver with a yellow handle had disappeared from the kitchen in mid-May.

Whiteway had never denied ownership of an axe or a knife but he used them, he said, only for target practice. He claimed not to know what had happened to the axe but said that he had lost the knife in the river. Although the knife was never found, the axe turned up in somewhat curious fashion.

It had for nearly a month been in the possession of a police officer. PC Arthur Cosh, a driver at Kingston, had been checking a patrol car on 18th June and had found it behind the rear seat and had put it in his locker. When Cosh returned to work after illness the axe had not been claimed and so he had taken it home and had chopped sticks with it. And then the penny dropped. . .

PC Cosh suddenly realised the significance of the axe. It had been in the police car which had taken Whiteway from Oxshott Heath to the police station. He at once reported the matter. Hannam was now able to send the axe to the laboratories for forensic testing; he had already sent some of Whiteway's clothing for tests. Although the axe produced a strong reaction to blood, its quantity was too minute to match for blood grouping. However, the blows to Christine's skull and Barbara's cheek matched the edge of the axe. And one of Whiteway's suede shoes, although it had been washed, was still heavily stained with blood in the eyelets and seams.

When Hannam and Sergeant Hudson interviewed their suspect at Brixton prison on 30th July, Whiteway strongly denied that he had ever had blood on his shoe. 'I don't believe it,' he said. 'I think you are putting one over on me.'

Whiteway acknowledged that the axe and the Gurkha knife which Hannam placed on the table were his. On the day he travelled in the police car, he said, he had been carrying the axe inside his coat. As he was sitting alone in the back of the car he hid it under the seat, believing that if it was found on him at the police station he might fall under suspicion for the towpath murders.

It was when the interview was over, and the detectives were

putting the statements and notes in their briefcases, that Whiteway asked, 'Were you kidding about the blood on my shoe?'

'I've explained to you,' Hannam replied, 'that one of your shoes had heavy bloodstaining on it.'

Up to then Whiteway had been sitting at the table but now he stood up, pale-faced and trembling.

Then he said, 'You know bloody well it was me, don't you? I didn't mean to kill them. I never want to hurt anyone.'

He agreed after a caution to dictate a statement.

'It's all up,' Whiteway said, the words spilling out. 'You know bloody well I done it, eh? That shoe's . . . me. What a bloody mess. I'm mental. I must have a . . . woman. I can't stop meself. I'm not a . . . murderer. I only see one girl. She came round the tree where I stood and I bashed her and she was down like a log. Then the other screamed out down by the lock. Never saw 'er till then, I didn't. I nipped over and shut her up. Two of them and then I tumbled the other one knew me. If it hadn't been for that, it wouldn't have happened. Put that . . . chopper away. It haunts yer. What more do they want to know. Why don't the doctors do something? It will be mental, won't it? I can't stop it. Give us it. I'll sign it.'

Whiteway was clearly shaken but then pulled himself together. 'Have you got the bike?' he asked.

Hannam replied that neither it nor Barbara's cycle had yet been found.

'So you've done it on me,' Whiteway shouted. 'I shall say it's all lies, like the blood. You can tear that last one [his statement] up. I did not give it.'

But the police now had his confession and Alfred Whiteway was to be committed for trial at the Old Bailey.

Odd that Barbara Songhurst's brother Danny should be married to a former girlfriend of Whiteway. She was astounded to hear of the charge. 'There's nothing like that about Alfy,' she said. 'He used to carry a knife. But he's not the sort of chap who would commit a murder. Why, he's a decent chap, much too fine a chap to do anything like that.'

And even Danny Songhurst was surprised. 'He's the last person to suspect in a case like this,' he said.

At the trial in October 1953, Mr Christmas Humphries for the prosecution argued that Barbara Songhurst lived near Whiteway's home and that they must have recognised each other. This, said counsel, was Whiteway's reason for killing her.

But the most dramatic moment came when Peter Rawlinson, defending counsel, cross-questioned Hannam about the statement that Whiteway had made and then retracted.

'What did you do to get Whiteway's signature?' he asked the policeman.

'I put the statement in front of him.'

'I suggest you put four signatures and four initiallings on several pieces of paper which you handed over to him.'

In other words, Whiteway had signed blank sheets.

'That is a terrible suggestion,' Hannam replied.

It was, Rawlinson suggested, 'a completely manufactured piece of fiction written by the officer'.

Then Rawlinson asked Hannam to sit down at the solicitor's table, trying to replicate what it had been like in Brixton prison when Whiteway had dictated his statement to the two detectives. This was a highly charged moment in court and it was apparent that Whiteway's fate depended on it.

Rawlinson sat at the table next to the detective. He handed Hannam a sheet of foolscap paper. Phrase by phrase, Rawlinson dictated the words of the statement to Hannam.

'It's all up,' he began, echoing the words of the accused. 'You know bloody well I done it, eh?' And more lines from the page, the detective scribbling them down until finally the policeman suddenly stopped writing and put down his pen. It was another dramatic moment.

'The atmosphere of that tense little room in Brixton prison, the outbursts from Whiteway, cannot possibly be conveyed in this court,' Hannam said. And Rawlinson had to concede that nothing could be gained by the experiment.

In the witness box Whiteway maintained that the statement was false and that he had been tricked into signing it. To the end he denied both murders.

The jury in this trial took only 45 minutes to reach a verdict of guilty and Alfred Whiteway hanged on 22nd December 1953.

Peter Rawlinson never forgave Hannam for 'swearing away a man's life'. But even if the evidence was thin – no knife found; no definite placing of Whiteway at the crime scene; a disputed confession – it cannot be doubted that the police had the right man. And had he not been caught when he was, would Whiteway have committed more murders? Was there a serial killer in the making here? The prosecution claimed that he had murdered Barbara Songhurst because she must have recognised him and Christine because she was there. But Whiteway's career suggests a man progressing from sexual assaults to murder. It does seem probable that he was caught just in time.

CRIME PASSIONEL?

It was a police helicopter that sighted the man, lying in a field near the house. He made no attempt to hide or run away when eventually police on the ground came to arrest him. He was in no condition to hide or run for he was in a drunken stupor. On the grass beside him were two nearly empty bottles, one of port, the other of whisky . . . and a bloodstained carving knife. It was a quick arrest, for the call about the murder had come only an hour or so earlier. But it was evident that the man needed urgent medical attention. He was suffering from alcohol poisoning.

When later he came round in hospital, he chose not to answer the police questions, muttering simply that he was 'very sad'. And undoubtedly he was.

What the police did know about him was that he was French and that his name was Gaeton Beissy. For the last nine months he had lived at the imposing South Holmwood mansion of the widowed 54 year old Carolyn Taylor. And now Mrs Taylor was dead, stabbed through the heart in her own kitchen. Her son, Mark, and daughter, Samantha, had reported her death shortly after it occurred, with the result that the police set up the search for Gaeton Beissy. And he was easily apprehended.

Three days after his arrest, Beissy attempted to kill himself by cutting his arms and wrists with the glass from his spectacles. Was this not indicative of his guilt? That at least is what the prosecution was to claim at both trials of the former light-aircraft pilot. Oh yes, both trials, for this was a less cut-and-dried matter than it first appeared to be.

And it begins as a romantic tale on a Mediterranean island when a wealthy and attractive widow met a handsome, dashing pilot. It may be that there is something about the pilots of small

Gaeton Beissy, the pilot.
(*Sunday Express*)

aircraft. What can it be? Do they carry some air of bravado about them? Do they remind us of buccaneers or soldiers of fortune? They are so different from the pilots of the very large commercial aeroplanes, the captains whose flight decks are a mass of computerised gadgetry. We certainly do not want a reckless streak in our package tour pilots. We do not want our scheduled aircraft pilots to have such dash. We want them to be solid, reliable chaps who won't take unnecessary risks, who will be responsible, have a due regard for rules. Whenever we glimpse them we seek reassurance from their demeanour. We look for the steadiness that we might at one time have sought from our bank managers. But it does seem that we have a more romantic view of those who fly older, more rickety little crates. They seem to have such flair. Are they really so full of derring-do or is it just our imagination? And was it such romantic notions about pilots that led Carolyn Taylor to fall in love with Gaeton Beissy? For Beissy was no captain of Concorde. He offered tourists to Corsica no more than short flips in his two-seater plane along the beaches, across the sea, over small towns and villages. This is not to say that Beissy was other than a good pilot. But he was also more than that. Or so it must have seemed to Carolyn the day he landed more or less opposite the restaurant where she was having lunch.

That was the September day in 1991 when Beissy came strolling over, handsome and, even at 56, quite dashing. That was the day when he and Carolyn first met, the day when the love affair began.

It is easy enough to condemn holiday romances, easy enough to say that they never last, that they are superficial and that mature people ought not to be overcome by their emotions. And yet, from what one can understand of the matter, the love affair between Carolyn Taylor from Surrey and Gaeton Beissy the Frenchman was sincere and deep. It was in that very sincerity and depth of feeling that the tragedy at South Holmwood had its origins.

Carolyn Taylor had come to Corsica to holiday with her 25-year-old daughter, Samantha. Eighteen months earlier, Harry Taylor, a dynamic and hugely successful businessman who had made his fortune out of property and fashion and to whom Carolyn had been married for nearly 30 years, died. Only now had she come to terms with her loss. At last she felt able to take some pleasure out of life. And now up stepped Gaeton Beissy, voluble, charming, debonair, rather exotic, a man seemingly at ease with the world. Once more Carolyn felt that life was worth living.

In October, when she returned to South Holmwood, Beissy went there with her. It is not possible to say what he expected, but the large, white, stone house, Taresmocks, was set well back in acres of woodland and at the end of a long drive. There were stables and horses here and Carolyn rode every day. It was an elegant life that Gaeton Beissy now lived. Not that he did not fit in, for he was a man of some urbanity. He seems to have got on well with Samantha, who lived in a cottage in the grounds and with Mark, the 23-year-old son, a motor engineer, still living at home. Perhaps the only feature that caused him some unease in the new circles in which he moved was that he spoke little English. He must have found that frustrating. He and Carolyn managed of course with their smatterings of common words. They had time enough, patience and love enough to make their meanings clear. But in the usual social whirl perhaps Gaeton felt rather left out unless he met someone who spoke some French. But the romance was still there as the nights lengthened into winter, as Christmas passed, and when spring and early summer came. Beissy was still deeply in love but was showing distinct signs of an obsessive possessiveness that Carolyn's friends noticed. Where had she been, he would ask. Whom had she seen, he would demand. Why had she been away so long? Every absence was queried. He was happy only in Carolyn's presence, increasingly resentful and suspicious whenever she was away from him.

If Carolyn began to have doubts about how this new relation-ship was going, these have not been revealed. But Samantha and Mark, who had at first welcomed their mother's renewed interest in life, began to experience some unease. When Carolyn gave her late husband's signet ring to Beissy, Mark had been upset. To him it must have seemed symbolic of a rejection of his father's memory. It cannot have been meant in this way, for Carolyn had loved Harry Taylor, but nevertheless Mark sensed it as a betrayal. There are suggestions too that Samantha now was less than enchanted with Beissy. Neither, however, ever suggested that the Frenchman was other than considerate and deeply devoted to their mother. He 'treated her like a queen'.

On 15th July 1992, nine months or so after she had introduced Gaeton Beissy into her home, Carolyn Taylor was stabbed to death in the kitchen at Taresmocks. And, despite two trials, how she met her death has not been established. Was she murdered in a savage rage by her lover, obsessed with the notion that she was sleeping with other men? Or was she killed accidentally by her son? In the kitchen that morning there were only three people – Carolyn, Mark and Gaeton Beissy – and the truth about what occurred is still obscure as far as the law is concerned.

The principal actors in the two trials gave significantly different acounts of what took place. It was simply a case of believing one man or the other. Hence there were two trials. But neither jury could agree on the veracity of what they were told.

Mark's account is that at 6.30 in the morning he was awakened by screams. At once he climbed out of bed and ran to his mother's bedroom, finding her naked and hysterical, her face a mask of blood. Her eyes were severely cut. She was heavily bruised and shaking. Through her tears she told Mark that Beissy had hit her repeatedly. 'The bastard has hit me with his fists,' she wept.

Mark told the court how he had tried to console his mother. He had washed her face, he said, and fetched her a T-shirt. They had gone down to the kitchen and from there Mark had telephoned the family doctor. He had just put down the receiver, when Beissy came into the kitchen, holding a carving knife behind his back. At the second trial John Nutting QC, for the prosecution, gave a starkly graphic account of what had occurred. 'As the defendant lunged towards Mrs Taylor with a knife he pushed the knife into her stomach, causing a dreadful wound to the woman he loved.

As Mrs Taylor pushed him away, or tried to do so, the defendant stabbed her again and she fell to the floor dying.'

The jury heard how Beissy had then put the knife to his chest and said to Mark. 'I've killed Carolyn. Kill me.' But only seconds later his mood had suddenly changed and he had then turned on Mark. 'I have killed your mother,' he said. 'Now I am going to kill you and Samantha. Your mother has been sleeping around.'

Beissy had raised the carving knife threateningly but the young man had managed to escape through the kitchen window. He ran to his sister's cottage from where he had telephoned the police.

Mark and Samantha had then decided to return to the house. Beissy was still there, squatting by Carolyn's body, still holding the knife. He had looked up when Samantha came in. He told her, 'I killed your mother because of you. It was all your fault.' He made a further threat but made no attempt to carry it out.

And now in all the confusion, the distress, the horror of the morning, Beissy slipped out of the house. The brother and sister waited for the arrival of the police.

Beissy's account differed significantly from Mark Taylor's. Speaking through an interpreter, he told the court that Carolyn had died in his arms after she was stabbed. But it was not he who had stabbed her, he claimed. It was Mark who had killed his mother and had then falsely accused her lover. Was the cause of the squabble between mother and son related to his anxiety about his inheritance, Mark was asked. He was to reply that his inheritance was of no interest to him. He had loved his mother and it was his mother's happiness that most concerned him.

In Beissy's version of events, on the morning of the killing he and Carolyn were roused at about six o'clock by Mark. There was something that he wanted to discuss, and Carolyn had asked Beissy to leave the bedroom while she talked to her son. To come to his mother's room at that time suggested he was concerned about something. It was Mark who set off the awful train of events according to Beissy.

Some time later Beissy found Carolyn and Mark in the kitchen. There had been an upset of some kind, a terrible upset. Mark was telephoning the doctor and his mother's face had been battered with punches. Beissy told how Mark had reached for a knife near the telephone and, seeing his movements and fearing his intentions, Carolyn tried to push past her son and place herself

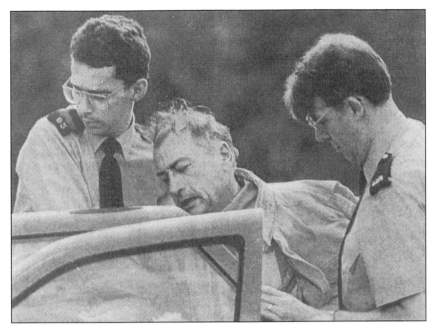

Gaeton Beissy being taken away by the police (Daily Express)

between him and her lover. And then Carolyn had screamed as the blood spurted on her breast. She had been stabbed. 'She turned herself around and held on to the breakfast bar,' Beissy told the court. 'She took two steps towards me. I held her behind her head and had my other hand around her body. Then I helped her to collapse.'

Two stories and two Old Bailey juries, sitting in February and May 1993, and no conclusion as to what exactly had occurred in the kitchen that summer morning. Neither jury could decide who had held the weapon which entered Carolyn Taylor's heart. Charges of murder and attempted murder against Gaeton Beissy were not proceeded with.

Was it an accident? Carolyn Taylor died when a knife penetrated her heart and lung. But there was a second wound revealed at the post-mortem and Mark Taylor had described seeing Beissy inflict two thrusts with the knife. Two stabs to the body scarcely seems like an accident.

After the jury was discharged, the judge, Mr Justice Lymbery advised Beissy to leave the country as soon as possible. Detectives who had presented the case said that as far as they were concerned it was now closed. They were not looking for anyone else in connection with this murder.

After the second trial Mark Taylor spoke of his mother. She was an exceptional woman, he said, and his best friend. She had never believed in violence. As for Beissy, he was horrified that he had walked free. 'For him to try to put the blame on me is unforgivable. I've been dragged through the mud.'

But the case remains unsatisfactorily concluded and inevitably the mystery it poses must linger. Accident? Murder? Regrettably, that will never now be legally resolved.

A DAY IN THE COUNTRY

Perhaps if June Benson had come out with it straight away, if she had said to her husband that she didn't really want to spend the day walking in Surrey because she didn't feel up to it, then the strange events on that July Sunday in 1954 would not have occurred. Or then again, would they have occurred to two other people? Difficult to say, really.

The Bensons – let's call them by the pseudonym used when their case was investigated and written up for the Society of Psychical Research – were antiques dealers in Battersea and they were seemingly quite exhausted by the amount of business they were doing. They both felt absolutely drained but made up their minds that on that Sunday they would get away from it all. But when she awoke, June Benson felt somewhat depressed. She felt more like spending a lazy day at home rather than making the effort to go out walking all day. But she thought that George would be disappointed and so she said nothing. Strange, isn't it, how things turn out? George felt exactly the same. He, too, felt lethargic. He, too, would just as soon have spent the day at home but like his wife he had not wanted to spoil their plans. So off they went to catch the train to Dorking, both suffering silently.

At Dorking they took the bus for Guildford, intending to get off at the Rookery, on the edge of Westcott, but somehow they missed the stop. Were they so tired that they slept on the bus? Whatever the case, they did get off at the next stop, Wotton Hatch. They were not too annoyed at their error. They knew the area well enough and were pleased to have the opportunity to call in at the church, St John the Evangelist, before the morning service. After all, this was the home of the multi-faceted John Evelyn, the 17th century diarist, scholar, and gardener – a man of the utmost

The Bensons visited this church before starting their climb up the hill.

fascination, and someone in whom the Bensons were already interested. They went into the church and then spent some time in the churchyard, looking at the weathered headstones, reading their faded inscriptions. And then it was time for their walk. That was why they had come, after all.

Turning right out of the churchyard, they made their way uphill, following a steep path between thick overgrown hedges. They seemed to climb for an age but at last they reached a grassy clearing at the top. There was a wooden bench and, their limbs aching from their stiff haul, they were grateful to sit down. It was already midday and they took out their sandwiches. Not that June had much appetite. She felt too numb, too heavy. She still had the sense of dullness that had oppressed her all morning. And there was an additional unease, though she could ascribe no reason to this. She sat there throwing crumbs for the birds, gazing with no great interest at the stretch of grass where they sat, at the woodland beyond and at the way the land fell sharply away to her right. From the distance, down in the valley, she could hear a dog barking and what sounded like someone chopping wood.

It was then that everything fell silent. No dog barked. No one chopped wood. There was no trembling of the boughs of the nearby trees. No birds sang. There was no background sound of traffic. It was not simply a peaceful silence. It was a dense silence, as if all sound had gone from the world. It was a silence beyond silence.

And suddenly June was chilled with a cold beyond cold. And she was afraid. George recalled her speaking, asking him if everything had gone cold. When he felt her arms she felt like a corpse.

All at once she was aware of three figures, standing in the clearing. They were dressed in black, she was to say later. She thought that they were in some kind of clerical robes but she was not specific about this, although she had no doubt that they were from some time in the past. But she did see their faces clearly. A round-faced man in the middle was friendly looking but those on each side of him wore expressions of absolute hatred. And what most terrified June about this was that the figures were not in front of her. They stood somewhere behind her, out of her line of sight. And she could not turn her head round to them for she was totally incapable of movement.

Then the apparitions disappeared and June gradually unfroze and was able to move once more.

George knew that June had undergone some inexplicable experience. He had not been aware of the apparitions but he did recognise the importance of getting June away. Something was wrong about this place and he hurried her down the slope in front of them. They eventually crossed a railway line but then both of them were overcome by fatigue. They lay down and both fell asleep.

In the early evening they found themselves in Dorking. 'Found themselves' sounds right, for neither of the Bensons could recall how it was that they reached the town. Had they caught the bus back? Had they walked? They had no recollection of events after lying down – and they acknowledged that going to sleep in such a totally unexpected manner was bizarre in itself – until arriving at Dorking railway station.

If George Benson did not experience the apparitions, he certainly was as fatigued as his wife and the details of the day's happenings escaped him just as they eluded her. He remembered the visit to the church and the stiff uphill climb, and it seemed to him that from that point the strangeness set in.

It had been so odd a day, and so unpleasant, that they did not return to that part of Surrey for some time. It was June who first went back. It was her curiosity that got the better of her, the strangeness of it puzzled her, and in 1956 she returned, hoping to make some sense of what had happened.

On June's return visit, the church was as before. How could it not be? But the walk . . . she turned to her right out of the church-yard as she and George had done two years earlier. But she could not find the path; that steep, straggly, overgrown path they had struggled up was nowhere to be found. And the land about was flat. The hill they had climbed, where was it? They had sat at the top but now . . . Perhaps she was mistaken. She went back to the churchyard, set off again, tried another way out, looked there for the path and the slope.

There were people about and she spoke to them. These were local people, who knew the area. But they knew of no path, no hill round there with a bench on top.

The following Sunday George went to Wotton to see if he could resolve the mystery. He met one of the congregation outside the church, a man who was woodman on the Wotton estate. Surely he would know the path, the hill, the clearing, the bench. But no, he did not. No such path, no such hill or clearing. And there were certainly no wooden benches on the estate.

And that left George and June completely mystified.

After some weeks the Bensons reported their mysterious adventure to the Society of Psychical Research, but at the time the Society was moving its premises and their case was mislaid and forgotten for nearly 20 years. It was not until 1973 that two members of the Society, Mary Rose Barrington and John Stiles, investigated the matter. They were in no doubt that the account the Bensons gave was sincere, that the couple had made their visit to Wotton church on the Sunday in July 1954 and that they had both undergone some unaccountable experience. They recognised George and June had shared much of the occurrence but that something extra had happened when June saw the apparitions.

That both the Bensons could have imagined the climb and the hill is not totally impossible. Such shared psychic experiences are recorded. Or were they really in this mysterious place in a true physical sense and then, in the course of a few hours, did they just as unaccountably return to Dorking?

Was this some trick of space? Is there another reality aside from the one in which we live? Had the Bensons stepped into some parallel world, some side by side existence, into a twin universe? And, lest this be thought absurd, perhaps it is sufficient to say that many scientists for the past hundred years or so have pondered the possibility of parallel dimensions.

Barrington and Stiles, in the course of researching this bizarre case, turned to John Evelyn's diary for a clue about the three figures in black. They found several entries relating to the trial of a group of men for conspiracy to assassinate the king. The entry for 15th March 1696 reads: 'Three of the unhappy wretches (whereof one a Priest) executed this weeke for intending to assassinate the King; acknowledging their intention, but acquitting K. James of instigating them to do it in that manner, and dying very penitently.' These three Jacobites were Edward King, Thomas Keyes and Robert Charnock, a priest and vice president of Magdalen College, Oxford, who performed the last offices. They were executed at Tyburn, hanged, drawn and quartered there. Can it have been these who appeared where the Bensons found themselves. Was Charnock the round-faced man with the friendly face? Had the Bensons' earlier visit to Evelyn's tomb something to do with the arrival of the three executed men in that phantom landscape? Were the Bensons, both of them feeling below par at the time, somehow strangely receptive to some psychic sensations in the church? Had they – or June at least – keyed in to Evelyn's personality and thus to his diary entry? Had Evelyn's thoughts about a spot he knew well and the three men he had written about projected themselves into the minds of the two visitors to the church? And did this then go beyond all logic and lead to the superimposition of the three men who had nothing at all to do with Wotton and who had never had direct dealings with John Evelyn onto the backcloth of that ever so odd site?

A day in the country for the Bensons – what a remarkable day. Not just a slip into another dimension of space but also of time. People involved in these time-space dislocations often appear to have some kind of premonition, a sense of foreboding and discomfort; they often remark on the sudden blanketing of sound; they lose all sense of time; they sometimes suffer a temporary paralysis and frequently are incapable of recalling fully the details of the experience. This seems to sum up much of what the Bensons said about their day out in the country.

THE BYFLEET POISONER

When Mabel Jones had her breakdown, she took her doctor's advice and went off to convalesce in Biarritz. Never mind that it was early January when she arrived there. Forget the fierce winds off the Atlantic, the temperatures still not much higher than those in England at that time of year, and reflect instead that in 1924 Biarritz was an elegant – and costly – resort. And forget that Mabel's breakdown was a result of her being recently declared bankrupt. She was not so short of cash that she could not stay at the Hotel Victoria. Her husband after all was still solvent, left behind to look after the hotel, the Blue Anchor, they had bought in Byfleet only a few months earlier.

How she intended to amuse herself is not at all clear. Whilst she might enjoy bracing seafront walks in the daytime, the nights must have been tiresome. Her French was almost non-existent and perhaps she frequently felt lonely. It would be surprising if she did not miss her children, a son of 18 and a 19 year old daughter. Perhaps in the long winter evenings after dinner, she was left much to herself, feeling herself to be an outsider. This is not to say that Mabel was not self-sufficient. After all, and unusual for those times, she had felt confident enough to travel alone to Biarritz.

Odd that the most sympathetic soul she got to know should be the hotel's wireless engineer, a 45 year old French Basque, whose duties were to give wireless concerts for the guests and to ensure that the wireless in the lounge worked. Every day the hotel's residents gathered to hear the broadcasts, faint and uncertain though they sometimes were. Only an expert wireless engineer could ensure good listening in those early days of broadcasting. And it was he, a man of undeniable charm and unbounded personal vanity, who was most pleasant to the English guest. And

Mabel Theresa Jones

how exotic he must have appeared to her, with his perfumed beard, his expressive gestures, his so un-English enthusiasms.

But if Mabel Jones was pleased to have made a new friend, she was unable to convey this to him. Nor could he speak to her, for he, Jean Pierre Vaquier, spoke no English. Impasse? Not at all. To overcome the language barrier, she bought an English-French dictionary.

He had been in the army, he was able to tell her, leafing the pages. In the war. Telegraphist. Engineer regiment.

She points to herself: formerly, she explains with the use of the dictionary, she possessed a cafe. Not now. The Old English Cafe. Richmond. She sold it. Then she bought the Blue Anchor.

He is divorced. After many years of marriage.

Her husband is at the Blue Anchor now. She has been ill and has come here to Biarritz to recover. She will stay several weeks.

He is an inventor, he says. He has invented a sausage-making machine. Don't laugh, he implores her. The sausage is so popular. In France, in Germany, in England. All over the world. The machine, it will make a fortune.

She may be doubtful about this. She has not yet told him, but a couple of years earlier she had a catering contract with the racetrack at Brooklands, which she had thought would make her fortune. But it all came to nothing. Shortly after arriving at the Blue Anchor, she was bankrupted.

Mabel and her Monsieur Vaquier meet in the hotel lounge, enjoying their exchanges. Within days they are taking lunch in bars and cafes.

They share their lives, their pasts, their secrets. Perhaps she even confesses that her husband is a drinker, a seriously heavy drinker. All in halting Franglais. He loves her, Vaquier says. And she loves him, she says; she loves her bushy-bearded Frenchman, her clever Frenchman, her dapper little Frenchman.

After two weeks Mabel left for Lourdes and Pau. But she would be back, she told him. And she did come back within days. And now together they went to stay as man and wife at the du Palais, the most elegant hotel in Biarritz, one of France's great hotels, built 50 years earlier by the Emperor Napoleon III as a palace for his wife, the Empress Eugénie. What splendour. Such exquisite rooms, such gracious stairways, such noble marble columns, such luxury. But when Mabel finally explained that she was bankrupt and when Vaquier responded that he – like all inventors – was at that time short of cash, they agreed to move on. This episode hints at something, a kind of inability to understand their own situation, as if their love blinded them to everything in the rational world. But suddenly, made to think about their financial position, they rustled up enough to pay their mounting bill and moved into the Hotel Bayonne, a more modest establishment.

Not that Vaquier seems to have been disheartened by this. He remained certain that one day the sausage-making machine would end all their troubles. But how happy they were now, these two middle-aged people, sharing a deep passionate love. They must have wished that it would continue for ever. But nothing lasts for ever. Mabel received a telegram from Alfred, her husband. She must come back. He was ill now. She'd have to take over running the Blue Anchor.

It was a bombshell. Mabel began her preparations for a premature return. Would she never see her little Frenchman again? And would he be for ever separated from Madame Jones, as he seems to have persisted calling her? The thought was unbearable to both of them. But could he not come to England? Would that not be possible? They shared this hopelessly romantic idea. So back they travelled north together, stopping at Bordeaux, and later in Paris. And then they parted, Mabel for Byfleet, Vaquier for Sens, where he would try, not for the first time, to sell the patent for his machine. Then, he promised, he would come to England.

Mabel arrived back at the Blue Anchor on 8th February. The following day, Vaquier signed in at the Russell Hotel in Russell Square. On 12th February he sent a telegram to Mabel. He was in England on business, he said. Would she and her husband join him for dinner that evening? No doubt they had planned this only days earlier. Alfred, however, was unwell and sent his apologies to his wife's new friend but Mabel agreed to come to London. At the Russell Mabel explained to her lover that Alfred was very poorly and that he intended to go to Margate for a few days.

That night Mabel returned to Byfleet and the next morning she saw off her husband to Margate. Then back she went to London. And that night she missed her return train to Byfleet and spent the night at the Russell. She went back to the Blue Anchor the following morning.

The chronology of what happened next is unclear, but it seems that later that day Vaquier arrived at Byfleet. And the couple had already concocted their tale. Mabel's son and daughter and the staff at the hotel were presented with the little Frenchman, whom she described accurately enough as her new friend, an inventor who was down on his luck temporarily. She would settle the bill of £8.8s.2d. at the Russell Hotel. But he had good prospects, Mabel reassured them. He had only to sell the patent.

Mabel gave her husband in Margate the same story. Vaquier had turned up short of cash, she told him on the telephone. Would it be all right to put him up for a while till he had sold the patent? And Alfred saw no reason to object. He had never met the man but if Mabel, his wife of nearly twenty years, said he was all right . . .

When Alfred Jones returned to Byfleet on 17th February, he was still very sick, his lungs heavily congested. The doctor called in to see him and ordered him to bed for two weeks. But gradually Alfred was up and about and making the acquaintance of Mabel's new friend. The men got on with each other very well. Vaquier was to say later that he had liked Alfred very much, regarding him

Jean Pierre Vaquier

as a brother. All three lunched together every day. In the evenings, Alfred retired early to bed leaving Mabel and Vaquier to dine alone.

Certainly at this period, the three new friends were discussing the future. Vaquier spoke of a villa to let in St Jean de Luz, not far from Biarritz. Why did Monsieur and Madame Jones not sell up here, get rid of the Blue Anchor, and move into the villa and open it up as a hotel and restaurant? It seems to have been a plan that they discussed with some enthusiasm, though it may be that gradually Alfred and Mabel had doubts about the feasibility of the proposal.

During this time Vaquier was paying visits to London, ostensibly to sell the patent. On 3rd March Mabel accompanied him to the Russell where they took a room but they returned to Byfleet in the evening. This was the last occasion on which they made love. Was Mabel beginning to weary of her new lover?

After all, how could the affair sustain itself in the close confines of the Blue Anchor, where sleeping with each other was out of the question. Vaquier certainly pressed Mabel to come away with him, though there is some debate about how often he asked her. Frequently, Mabel was to say. Only once, said Vaquier, when he saw how unhappy her marriage was. Was Mabel now beginning to regret the presence of a man she had thought the love of her life? Was there some cooling off? Was the Frenchman's charm wearing thin? Was there some dawning suspicion that he was a sponger? Was he now no more than a nuisance? George Whitewick, the hotel manager, was of the view that Mabel was increasingly resentful of her holiday lover.

What is difficult to decide is what precisely were the feelings of Vaquier and Mabel on the morning of 29th March, the morning when Alfred Jones died an unimaginably terrible death. Had they now no amorous inclinations? Later they were both to distance themselves, each from the other, but it would be interesting to know if on that most awful morning they still desired each other, if there was still some residue of that passion which had thrown their lives so adrift.

As usual Vaquier was downstairs early that morning, making coffee for himself. Today, the only change from the Frenchman's customary routine was that he took his coffee in the bar-parlour. Odd that, for it reeked of the previous night's drinking, which had gone on later than usual, as the Joneses had held a boozy gathering for their friends and the room had not been cleaned. And furthermore it was chilly in there, for there was no heating.

Why on earth did he not go into the coffee-room as he usually did? It was warm in there, for there was a gas fire and the room was not in need of cleaning. George Whitewick and the cook, Elizabeth Fisher, both showed annoyance that he should be in a room that they wanted to clean, but Vaquier would not budge, pretending not to understand what it was they wanted. Even when Alfred Jones came down to do the accounts for the previous day, he failed to persuade his guest to move from his armchair. Was there some reason for all this?

Was it that he wanted easy access to the bottle of bromo salts which was in its usual place on the mantelpiece? Alfred had now to some extent overcome the illness which had laid him low the previous month and had immediately resumed his old heavy drinking habit. It was his custom to try to settle his stomach with a glass of the salts. Mabel was now in the bar-parlour, sitting with the dog in her lap. Vaquier was in the armchair. Waiting? Alfred reached for the bottle, poured the salts into a glass of water and stirred the contents.

'Oh, God,' he said, as he swallowed the mixture. 'They're bitter.'

Mabel picked up the bottle and poured out some into her hand. 'They've been tampered with,' she said.

Straightaway she filled a glass with common salt and water and gave it to her husband. Then she made tea for him. And then he began to vomit violently. And then the pains began.

Colic, perhaps, their visitor suggested.

But now Alfred was staggering round the room, acutely ill. Together, George Whitewick and Vaquier carried him upstairs and put him to bed.

But Alfred's condition was worsening by the minute. His whole body was twitching. His muscles contracted. He found it difficult to breathe. Now his back formed a rigid arch, supported on the bed only by his head and heels.

When Dr Carle arrived in response to Mabel's telephone call, he saw Alfred Jones's tortured frame go through a series of convulsions, temporarily subsiding before another onset of the most excruciating pain. At times, Alfred mercifully lost consciousness but then he would awaken once more to the most agonising spasms.

And finally the patient died. Dr Carle had been unable to do anything for him. Death, merciful when it came, was in the doctor's view a consequence of poisoning. And he guessed which poison it might be. For it is strychnine which condemns its victims to such unbearable tortures.

Alfred had taken salts, the doctor learnt. He asked for the bottle. It was brought to him. He sniffed it. He held it up to the light. He tipped it to his finger and the thinnest thread of liquid trickled out. He tasted it, recognising the trace of bitterness. Yes, someone had tampered with the bottle he was sure. And someone had tried unsuccessfully to rinse away all trace of the poison. He sent for the glass tumbler and the spoon which Alfred had used. The three items were sent away for analysis. They were all three to show signs of strychnine.

It is remarkable that no one was charged with this murder for nearly three weeks. After all, it was likely that the poisoner was in the house but no one was taken for other than routine questioning about the facts. Indeed only minutes after Alfred's death, Mabel accused Vaquier of the murder. Marcella Whitewick, who with her husband acted as manager at the hotel, was present and recalled Vaquier falling to his knees in tears. 'Oh God, Madam,' he is alleged to have sobbed, 'you accuse me?' And later, when she again accused him, he was said to have admitted his crime to her. 'Yes, Mabs,' he said. 'For you.' Yet if this admission was ever made, Mabel did not go immediately to the police.

But Vaquier was certainly made to feel that his presence was no longer welcome at the Blue Anchor. Even so it was the police who suggested to him that perhaps he would find it in the circumstances more agreeable to move to the Railway Hotel in Woking.

Here was a poisoning which intrigued the country. Journalists besieged the Blue Anchor, and Vaquier in Woking posed for photographs, revelling in the publicity. Perhaps they paid him for his contributions. That seems highly likely, for Vaquier was not earning at the time and he had as yet failed to sell the patent of the sausage machine.

Similarly at interviews with the police he said that the murder had been committed by 'a coward, jealous of my presence there'. Whom could he mean? Who was jealous of him? He suggested that one day he would reveal the name of the murderer. The poison, he said, had been 'put in by the servant in the pay of this rascally suitor'. Who could possibly be the servant who had poisoned the salts? And who was the 'cowardly suitor'? He had even said that he thought 'the second act of the drama will be the disappearance of the wife of George'. The wife of George? This was a reference to Marcella Whitewick. But why should she disappear? In all, the Frenchman made five statements voluntarily to Superintendent Boshier. How unwise. For Boshier over the days had more and more understanding of the man who so generously offered his opinions.

But it was all fascinating stuff. How the reporters loved this eager foreigner who offered himself so freely. 'A photo, sir?', they asked him, and Vaquier preened himself. Of course, a photo.

It was the photo of Vaquier which so astonished Horace Bland, a pharmacist in Southampton Row. For he recognised the man staring so proudly out of the newspaper. It was one of his customers. It was the Frenchman. He had called in for purchases several times some weeks ago. But he had not been called Vaquier. Bland looked up the poisons register. There was the date, the printed name, the signature, the address. 'J. Vanker', staying at the Russell Hotel, had on 1st March purchased 20 grammes of perchloride of mercury and .12 of a gramme of strychnine. Bland, a French speaker, had at first been uncertain about selling the poison to his customer but he had been reassured that it was essential for his wireless experimentation. The man was a wireless expert, that much was evident, and the pharmacist had eventually accepted that strychnine was used in wireless telegraphy.

But now, seeing the photograph, Horace Bland knew that 'J. Vanker' was somehow involved in the infamous poisoning case at Byfleet. He went to the police. On 19th April Jean Pierre Vaquier was arrested and charged.

Vaquier's four-day trial began at Guildford Assizes on Wednesday 2nd July. It was a fascinating occasion. What about Mabel Jones, asked Sir Henry Curtis Bennett, defence counsel for Vaquier. Was she as straightforward a witness as she purported to be? Was she not, like her husband, a heavy drinker? Did she not take part in riotous parties at their hotel? After her husband's death did she not dance with reporters who came to the hotel? And had she not another lover? And had she not, two weeks before Alfred's death, given him back her wedding ring? When Mr Justice Avory asked if any of this questioning was relevant to the case Bennett responded that it was intended to prove that Mabel Jones was not a woman whose testimony could be relied upon.

Mabel, not unnaturally, denied most of the damaging implications of the questions. The suggestion of another lover really does seem to be highly unlikely and there is doubt about the propriety of other questions.

The court learnt from the Attorney General, Sir Patrick Hastings, who led for the prosecution, how before the doctor's arrival Mabel had taken the bottle into the kitchen. Hastings indicated Vaquier's desperation at this stage to get hold of the bottle in order to get rid of the remaining strychnine. But he did not know precisely where Mabel had put it and, when she was upstairs with her husband, Vaquier had dashed in to the cook, Elizabeth Fisher. 'Medicine – doctor – quick,' he had called out to her. She assumed that the doctor wanted to look at the salts that Alfred Jones had taken and pointed out to Vaquier the kitchen drawer that Mrs Jones had put it in. Vaquier had immediately retrieved the bottle and rinsed it out. But he had not been thorough. There were still traces of strychnine in the bottle when it was inspected by the doctor.

Under cross-examination, Vaquier introduced for the first time the story of Mabel Jones's other lover. Bruce Millar, the Joneses' solicitor, was the 'cowardly suitor' who had induced Vaquier to purchase the strychnine. Millar had told Vaquier he wanted to kill a dog and at the time strychnine was sometimes used for this purpose. Millar had explained to Vaquier that he did not have time to visit a pharmacy. Furthermore, according to Vaquier, Millar had suggested that he use a false name and address for his purchase. Nobody ever gave his right name in these circumstances, Millar had assured him. Hence, Vaquier had given his name as Vanker and his address as the Russell Hotel at a time when he was living in Byfleet.

Once he had the poison, Vaquier said, he had handed it over to Millar. Only later did he realise that the solicitor had his reasons for wanting to be rid of Alfred Jones. But he did not do the deed himself. That was left to the manager, George Whitewick. He had not wanted to move to France as Vaquier and the Joneses were proposing. This was one way of stopping it.

And what about the mysterious suggestion that the next person to disappear from the scene would be Marcella Whitewick? Well, she had wanted to go to France and so she too was to be put out of the way, presumably by George.

But in the end, despite his convoluted tale, Jean Pierre Vaquier was found guilty and sentenced to hang.

But the tale did not end there. Only days after sentence Vaquier asked to speak to the governor at Wandsworth prison, where he awaited execution. He said that one day while he was staying at the Blue Anchor he had seen a woman – either Mabel Jones or Marcella Whitewick but he could not be certain – go to a toolshed in the garden of the hotel. He had been curious and had later visited the toolshed. To his surprise he had found two bottles of strychnine there, hidden in the wall behind a loose brick. There was enough strychnine to kill over 700 people. He had not bought the poison in such a quantity.

The police searched the toolshed and found the bottles with their terrifying amounts of poison, just as Vaquier had said. And truly none of it could be traced to the Frenchman. Certainly Horace Bland had sold him enough to kill four people. He had admitted to that but this quantity was of a totally different order. Who wanted, who needed, such an amount? If Vaquier, why did he need to buy such a relatively modest amount from Bland. And how had he known of such a convenient place to hide the strychnine? But if not Vaquier, then who had put it there?

But none of this saved the Frenchman. His appeal failed and he was executed on 12th August, eight eventful months or so since he had met Mabel Jones, the woman for whose love, it does seem, he committed that most awful, cruel murder.

Patricia Hastings' book about her father offers us an interesting sidelight on this case. 'Pat never took a murder case if he could possibly avoid it and only once was he Prosecuting Counsel in one of these,' she wrote. 'This was inevitable as it was a Crown Prosecution against the Frenchman Vaquier, which happened when Pat was Attorney General and he found the accused so detestable that he was not unduly distressed when the man was convicted.'

That may say something about Hastings. It certainly says something about Vaquier, that vain exhibitionist, that rather stupid little man, who committed a most hideously cruel murder and then tried to implicate others.

THE EWELL KIDNAPPING

Perhaps the greatest mystery of all is human behaviour. You never can tell what people are going to do next. If we just bore in mind the simple notion that there is nothing quite beyond our fellow humans in terms of irrationality and stupidity, then we should never be surprised. But they do surprise us and it is often difficult to work out why they behave as they do.

Take Joyce McKinney and Kirk Anderson. What a godsend to the tabloids they were. He was a fairly passive character in the drama that in 1977 and 1978 intrigued and titillated the newspaper-reading public. A handsome young man, he was shy and gangling in a James Stewart sort of way. And she was a blonde beauty queen who had represented Wyoming in 1967 and the USA in the Miss World contest of 1973. And the fact was that she had him kidnapped in Ewell and taken to a secret hideaway in Devon. With its naturally shy male and its notably un-shy curvaceous blonde – 'curvaceous' is not my word: blame the press – this had all the hallmarks of a top-class cinema comedy. Only in the end it did not turn out happily for those involved. Still, it entertained the nation for a while.

And in the end, when the one-time school cheer-leader and her male accomplice skipped the UK, posing as a pair of deaf-mute mime artists, the nation was entertained even more. And then she turned up in Georgia, where she had been hiding out, disguised as a nun. What rollicking fun for all those who did not seem to realise this was a case of rape. If it had been the other way around, matters might have been different but, as it was a man who had been whisked away as an object of desire, no one seemed particularly to mind. What people seemed to enjoy was the sheer crackbrained nature of the whole escapade.

Kirk Anderson was a shy, gangling young man.

The character in all of this affair who remains shrouded in mystery is Keith May, the accomplice who actually pointed the gun at Kirk Anderson and forced him into the car in which, back in the shadows, sat the hypercharged Joyce. Then it was off to the Devon cottage near Okehampton, where for three days the allegedly shell-shocked Kirk was held. Keith May was there throughout and it is his part in the venture which is inexplicable. Why did he get himself involved in such an obviously oddball happening? Why did a personable young man, a trainee architect, an American like the other two in this overheated affair, take the part he did? He was to say that it was because he was such a friend of Joyce. But to link himself to such an extraordinary enterprise seems to have been taking friendship rather further than might normally be expected. He also claimed that he was hoping to rescue Kirk from the Mormons, though Kirk himself never indicated any desire for release. Keith May's participation remains a mystery in this bizarre tale.

Joyce McKinney had started out boy-shy, she was to say. She had never drunk or smoked and in fact became known around the school campus as 'Little Miss Perfect'. (Many years later she was to be commemorated somewhat satirically in a song of that title by the punk rock group 'Demon Preacher'.) It was at Brigham Young University in Salt Lake City, when she was 27 that she first clapped eyes on a fellow drama student, the 6 ft 4 ins Kirk Anderson. Until now, shy and retiring – this was Joyce's view of herself – she had kept students at arm's length. And anyway, most of them were too young for her. But now she was entranced by the man she said was so handsome that he put Paul Newman to shame.

Kirk was soon ensnared. 'We were together constantly,' Joyce told the Epsom magistrates, 'but we did not have intercourse. He teased me and kissed me until I was out of my mind.' They had met only a few times when she lured the diffident and awkward student onto her water-bed. In some of her versions Joyce said that they made love and she was later to excuse her behaviour by saying that she had conceived and miscarried as a consequence of the liaison. It was such a torrid affair, Joyce said. 'It was bombs, fire crackers, the fourth of July every time he kissed me.'

Torrid or not, Kirk denied ever having had intercourse with Joyce. He admitted to having transgressed the Mormon code. Like all of their unmarried missionaries, he had sworn a vow of celibacy and he had certainly not broken it. Yes, he admitted to too close an attachment, but intercourse? Never. He had refused her begging him to go further but he admitted that he had broken the rules 'by becoming involved with Miss McKinney; by being alone with her; by holding her in his arms; by having sexual relations with her; and by using her first name.' The admission of 'sexual relations' was not, however, intended as an admission of full intercourse.

Consumed by guilt about the shenanigans on the water-bed and elsewhere, Kirk then sought out his bishop and confessed to what had happened. There was only one solution. He must break off their brief affair. But Hell hath no fury . . . Incensed at the snub, Joyce quit the Mormons whom she held to be responsible for the unhappy state of things and started a campaign against the man who so obsessed her. His house windows were smashed, his tyres ripped and a car he was driving rammed. Referring again to the bishop, Kirk was advised to flee and was posted by the church to California. And Joyce followed. There was further harassment.

Then, Oregon; and here came Joyce yet again. After two years' further torment, abroad offered the only possibility.

In early 1977 Kirk Anderson was in East Grinstead, starting a two year posting as a door-stepping missionary. But good private investigators can find out pretty well anything. They were able to tell Joyce exactly where he was. He then moved to Reading. No good. Here was Joyce again. Finally Kirk moved to the Mormon temple in Banstead Road in Ewell.

One September morning a stranger approached Kirk outside the Ewell Church of the Latter Day Saints. Could he have a word, the stranger asked. He was thinking of joining the Mormon church and wondered if Kirk could advise him. Then out came the gun, prodded into the unsuspecting young man's stomach. He was bustled into a waiting car and a blanket was thrown over his head. He spent the five-hour journey on the floor of the vehicle, uncertain what was going to happen to him. After all, his knowledge of Joyce McKinney was enough to tell him that at best her reactions were unreliable. What on earth could he expect? He was on a journey to some unspecified place in the company of a woman he had spurned and a mysterious stranger who had threatened him with a gun.

The Devon cottage was remote and, in Joyce's words, 'real romantic'. Here Kirk was well treated, she said. The cottage was cosy and she prepared all the meals. It was idyllic. And she was going to release him, she told Kirk. He had nothing to fear. He'd get home. Just as soon as he promised to marry her. And he had to give her a baby. 'All I really wanted was to see his little blond-haired babies running round my home,' Joyce later admitted.

But he was tied up, Kirk claimed. In fact he was fastened to the bed by a 10 ft chain and a leather strap.

On the third night Joyce, wearing her negligee, came into the bedroom and put some music on the tape recorder. She lay on the bed beside him. She asked him if there was anything he wanted. Yes, he had answered, he wanted a backrub. When Kirk Anderson related the account to the Epsom magistrates, they did query it. Given the circumstances – the music, the bed, the woman in the negligee – was it not, they asked, an erotic, sexually suggestive request to make and bound to tempt her? Anderson did not think so. 'I do not look at a backrub like that. My Mom gives me a pretty good backrub but that does not mean that I want sex with her.' Is this really very convincing?

At one point, Kirk Anderson claimed to have lost his temper with the persistent Joyce. He tried to throw her off the bed but he knew it was no good, he said. 'She said she was going to get what she wanted whether I wanted to or not.'

Kirk claimed that she now tore off his pyjamas and had May spreadeagle him, his hands and feet tied to the four quarters of the bed. Then, she took off another article of his clothing, little known about by the non-Mormon public. This was the one-piece undergarment, regarded as sacred, which served as some sort of male chastity belt. As she had desecrated the garment, Anderson later burnt it.

Joyce admitted to the chaining of her loved one. But, despite what he said, he was a willing participant in what then occurred. She did no more than stimulate him. These were no more than bondage games. They were having a 'fun time down in Devon'. Kirk had enjoyed himself, every minute, Joyce said. 'If he had not been willing, this little 120 pound girl could not have tied up a 250 pound, 6 ft 4 ins man,' she told the magistrates. 'His legs are as big around as my waist.' He had simply revelled in all that had occurred, lying on the bed 'grinning like a monkey'.

Joyce explained the necessity of tying up her lover.'Kirk has to be tied up to have an orgasm,' she announced. 'I cooperated because I loved him. I put ropes and fake blood on him, tore off his pyjamas and said "Oh, you sexy tiger." Once he was tied up he attained sexual satisfaction.'

This wasn't a matter of coarse lust. Joyce said that when she was in Utah she had sent up prayers for 'a very special boy' to come into her life. Kirk Anderson was the answer to that prayer. Then she made the statement that the press simply fell upon. 'I loved Kirk so much,' she told the world, 'I would have skied down Mount Everest in the nude with a carnation up my nose.'

How the press loved it all. *The Daily Mirror* and the *Daily Express* obtained a photograph of her in the nude, while the *Sun* had to be content to stick her head on the body of a naked woman skiing down snowy slopes with a carnation in her nose. But what copy.

The *Sun* gabbled, 'The gospel according to Mormon sex-in-chains girl Joyce McKinney is: Give a man what he wants. I'm a

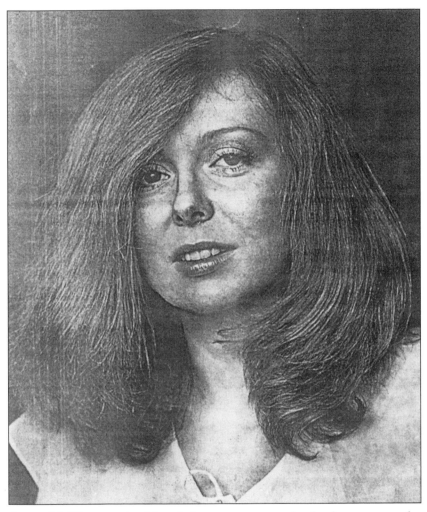

Joyce McKinney, the blonde beauty queen who had represented the U.S.A. in the 1973 Miss World contest.

very old-fashioned girl. I believe that a man's home is his castle and a husband should be pampered. All I wanted to do with Kirk was to satisfy and pleasure him. But he had deep inhibitions due to his upbringing. I wanted to get rid of those guilt feelings by doing sexually outrageous things to him in bed. I thought I had succeeded but in the end the Mormon church won.'

So why did Kirk Anderson deny that he had enjoyed his three days in Devon? According to Joyce, he was lying because he feared excommunication from the Mormon church.

In the end, after the third day, and after promising to marry her, Kirk was driven back to London and released. From there he returned to his home in Milton Gardens, Epsom, by train. By then he had been in touch with the police.

Joyce McKinney and her mysterious accomplice, Keith May, were arrested two days later. They were charged with abduction, unlawful imprisonment and possessing an imitation .38 revolver. Then came the information that Joyce had entered Britain on a false passport. On her way to the committal proceedings in September 1977, she protested her innocence and handed out messages written on pages of the Bible. One of these read: 'Please ask Christians to pray for me.'

Out of these proceedings came the tale about the depths of her love and how it had led to the kidnapping of Kirk Anderson. The police strenuously opposed bail – principally because of the variety of names she assumed – and she and her accomplice were remanded in custody. The trial was fixed for the following May.

Because of anxieties about her health, McKinney and May were granted bail in March, two months prior to the scheduled date for the trial. In April, Joyce McKinney and Keith May were nowhere to be found. Carrying false passports, they had skipped the country, disguised as deaf-mute performers. Then there was a period in the Appalachians in some or other disguise and the final unmasking in Georgia, where Joyce wore a nun's habit.

And over the months more of the story came out. One friend told how Joyce had visited skin flicks and live sex acts in order to pick up tips on arousal. She had also placed an advertisement in an underground paper asking for: 'A muscle man, a pilot and a preacher to help in a romantic adventure.' This team never assembled but she did manage to finance the trip to England with $15,000 given to her by an insurance company for injuries received in a car crash. On the other hand, according to other press reports, she had once earned $25,000 working as a nude mud-wrestler and porn model. Whether true or not, there is no doubt that when she had arrived at Heathrow with Keith May in August 1977 she was carrying her wedding dress, several honeymoon nighties, a £1,000 wedding ring, £5,500 and

Joyce appeared in Georgia dressed as a nun.

handcuffs, which she was to say were mink-lined as she had no wish to hurt her love. She had taken the tip about the fur lining, she said, from a sex manual. Joyce had also been in possession of a false passport and other documents in eight different names. And as they escaped from Britain so easily, she obviously had other false documents of which the police were unaware. She was sure that he really loved her. 'If I did not have faith in his love for me, I could not have flown halfway round the world with my wedding ring and my trousseau in my suitcase to see him.'

Oddly enough the proposals to bring her and Keith May back

to Britain to stand trial were dropped. Rape case or not, the authorities must have thought it not worth worrying about.

In 1984 police picked Joyce up outside the airline offices where Kirk was then working. She had a notebook listing his activities, photographs of his home, and in her car boot, a rope and handcuffs. She was only checking that he was happy, she told police. She had wanted to see him just for old time's sake. According to her lawyer, Joyce was writing a screenplay about her experiences and 'wanted to find out how the story ended'.

The mystery of human behaviour indeed! One may be able to work out what it was that drove Joyce McKinney. There are a number of opinions about her motives. But what of Keith May, that shadowy figure? What was he up to? Is it really true that he was trying to save Kirk Anderson from what he regarded as a dangerous cult? Men with revolvers who support an enterprise of this kind are not really the best authority on what may or may not be sound behaviour. And after all, what was he doing all those hours when Kirk Anderson was chained to the bed? What was he up to when Joyce was seducing the man in chains? One of the papers ran a headline: 'My sex in chains ordeal at the hands of Madam Mayhem'. Didn't Keith May see it in that light?

Anyway, a year or two ago, the one-time student architect was said to be selling plumbing supplies in Los Angeles. Kirk Anderson was last heard of as a travel agent and separated from the Mormon girl he married after his return from the United Kingdom. Joyce McKinney lives as a recluse on her smallholding in the mountains on the border of North Carolina and Tennessee. Most recent reports say that she is not in good health. Nor apparently does any man figure in her life.

BIBLIOGRAPHY

Alexander, Matthew *Tales of Old Surrey* Countryside Books 1985
Barrington, Mary Rose *A Slip in Time and Place* Fate Magazine Oct 1985
Bord, Janet and Colin *Modern Mysteries of Britain* Grafton Books 1987
Evelyn, John *Diary Vol. 5* Oxford 1955
Fodor, Nandor *The Unaccountable* Award Books 1968
Fodor, Nandor *The Haunted Mind* Signet 1968
Gaute, J.H.H. and Odell, Robin *Murder 'WhatDunit'* Pan 1984
Goodman, Jonathan (Ed.) *The Railway Murders* Sphere 1986
Gribble, Leonard *Adventures in Murder* John Long 1954
Janaway, John *Surrey Murders* Countryside Books 1988
Jenkinson, Sally *Ash and Ash Vale: A Pictorial History* Phillimore 1990
Lane, Brian *Encylopaedia of Forensic Science* Headline 1992
Mackenzie, Andrew *The Seen and the Unseen* Weidenfeld and Nicolson 1987
Mackenzie, Andrew *Adventures in Time* The Athlone Press 1997
Morton, James *A Calendar of Killing* Warner Books 1996
Shortland, Edward *The Murder of Station Sergeant Thomas Green* Actel (Undated)
Tullett, Tom *Murder Squad* The Bodley Head 1979
Webb, Duncan *Deadline for Crime* Mulle 1955

The author has also consulted a wide range of national and local newspapers and magazines.